HARD FIGHTING SOLDIER

ENDORSEMENTS

The Highland Church of Christ began their long partnership with Joe and Rosa Belle in 1971 when they initiated a new work in Papua New Guinea. This became a friendship which extended more than 40 years, to the very end of their lives. My life has been greatly enriched by the friendship, teaching, and exemplary model of what a praying Christian looks like. Joe and Rosa Belle were two ordinary people who took the hand of God and courageously walked through the adventures chronicled in this book. As a result they are extraordinary examples of what God will do through those who are fully committed to Him.

By reading this book, you will be blessed by the research, interviews, papers, and prayers that Joe and Rosa Belle left behind as a challenging legacy for us.

Larry McKenzie
Highland Church of Christ, Cordova, Tennessee

David Sitton's book accurately captures the vivacity of the Cannons, the humor and heartache they experienced in life, along with the challenges and exultant victories won for Christ through their ministry. From Japan, to Okinawa, to Papua New Guinea, to Memphis, Tennessee, to Indonesia and Belarus, to the Ukraine, and finally to glory—follow the unfolding story of Joe Cannon's heroic adventures that will bring chuckles and tears and inspiration to live more authentically in our faith!

With evident admiration and respect, but with frankness and humor, David Sitton tells the compelling story of Joe Cannon, truly a *Hard Fighting Soldier* for his Lord. Joe's endless energy, his irrepressible humor, his empathetic response to the poor, his rugged spirit and boundless faith, marked him as a missionary of outstanding proportions.

Geoffrey H. Ellis
Waterloo, Ontario, Canada

I met Joe Cannon in Okinawa, Japan in 1965, and we remained close friends until his death. Joe was the type of Christian one might be fortunate enough to meet only once or twice in a lifetime. He was a man who epitomized faith in motion and was truly willing to die for the gospel. He was the real deal missionary. Over the long years of our friendship I saw him disappointed many times, but I never once saw him discouraged! *Hard Fighting Soldier* will encourage your faith as you read the highlights and the lowlights in the life of one of God's missionaries to the world. God, send us more Joe Cannons.

Don Brown
Texarkana, Texas

What a wonderful book this is! I knew Joe Cannon and his family in Okinawa, Memphis, and Papua New Guinea, and my father, the late Bob Herndon, and Joe were close friends. David Sitton has done a masterful job in portraying this incredible character and his astonishing life. Joe had a huge influence on me, as he did on so many others, and I'm glad to see his story told for a broader audience.

Ernest Herndon, author and photographer
Outdoors Editor (*Enterprise-Journal*), Gloster, Mississippi

David Sitton has done a wonderful job of telling the story of an outstanding and unique missionary couple. I was a senior at Harding when Joe arrived and taught there during his senior year in 1943. Later I visited him several times in Japan. It is good to reminisce my association with a humorous, capable and dedicated man of God and to learn more of his achievements.

Dr. Clifton L. Ganus, Jr.
President, Harding University (1965-87)
Chancellor-Emeritus, Harding University, Searcy, AR

I have watched America change from the "Greatest Generation" to the "Millennials" of our present day. God transcends such changes but works through them. Joe Cannon stands as one of a number of examples of what God does to lay foundations that last for generations. The sheer guts and determination of such unfettered faith puts my generation to shame. But thank God we have such shoulders to stand on. Read this story to understand what we have been handed.

Robin Cannon (Joe's son)
Austin, Texas

Joe Cannon (Uncle Joe) was a part of my life since before I was born. He married my father's youngest sister and introduced my parents to each other. He was funny and fearless. He was relentless in seeking to help the poorest of the poor. He was a man of prayer and of passion. I'm pretty sure that anyone who met Uncle Joe never forgot him. I am grateful for his example of love and devotion, and I'm so glad that more people will get to meet Uncle Joe through this book.

Kathleen (Kathy) Cannon Straker
Houston, Texas

Wonderful! is the best thing I can say about David Sitton's book about Joe Cannon. If you thought you knew the hard-fighting soldier, just have a look at his other self: the kind, thoughtful, loving, forgiving, inspiring, soft-hearted true gentleman you'll discover in this un-put-downable biography.

Betty (Dollar) Cannon
Missionary and Widow of Joe Cannon

Hard Fighting Soldier is so captivating I read it in one sitting. Joe Cannon's burning desire to take the gospel to those who had not heard it was apostolic in its intensity, and David Sitton's record of it makes the reader feel like he/she is sitting in the Book of Acts. The text is well-written and well-documented. This book has a divine purpose of inspiring a slumbering, culturally comfortable church to bold, faith-driven action. I only wish it could have been available 50 years ago—while it was being lived out in Joe's and Rosa Belle's life. May God grant it wide circulation throughout our brotherhood, and may it spill over into the lives of all believers everywhere. It will bless—and disturb—all who read it.

James S. Woodroof
Author of *The Church in Transition*

If Joe Cannon isn't the Apostle Paul of our generation, he should be a candidate!

Jimmy Allen
Author and Harding University Professor (Retired)
Memphis, Tennessee

HARD
FIGHTING
SOLDIER

JOE CANNON:
65 YEARS OF PIONEER GOSPEL
EXPLOITS FOR THE GLORY OF GOD

DAVID SITTON

AMBASSADOR INTERNATIONAL
GREENVILLE, SOUTH CAROLINA & BELFAST, NORTHERN IRELAND

www.ambassador-international.com

Hard Fighting Soldier

Joe Cannon: 65 Years of Pioneer
Gospel Exploits for the Glory of God

Printed in the United States of America

ISBN: 978-1-62020-211-1
eISBN: 978-1-62020-310-1

Cover design: Matt Taylor and Justin Vander Ark
Typesetting: Hannah Nichols and Justin Vander Ark
E-book conversion: Anna Riebe

AMBASSADOR INTERNATIONAL
Emerald House
427 Wade Hampton Blvd.
Greenville, SC 29609, USA
www.ambassador-international.com

AMBASSADOR BOOKS
The Mount
2 Woodstock Link
Belfast, BT6 8DD, Northern Ireland, UK
www.ambassadormedia.co.uk

The colophon is a trademark of Ambassador

DEDICATION

When I die, throw a gospel meeting and forget about me!

Joe Cannon

Less than a year before Joe died, I enjoyed half a day with him in his living room in Memphis.

Three times, in various ways, he repeated this sentiment. Finally, I asked him what he thought about me writing his biography. He barked back: "Promote Missions!"

Joe Cannon was a missionary, heart and soul. He pushed the gospel forward, squeezing more juice out of every mile and minute than any man I've ever known or known about. He devoted nearly 65 years to going with the gospel of Christ across some of the toughest terrain, through the severest of life's sorrows, among some of the earth's most challenging peoples.

The biography of such a man should be dedicated to the aim of his ambition:

GET THE GOSPEL PREACHED AMONG ALL NATIONS

My life is worth nothing to me, if only I may finish the race and complete the task the Lord Jesus has given me, the task of testifying to the gospel of God's grace.[1]

SPECIAL THANKS

Betty and Robin Cannon for the loan of a treasure trove of more than 60 years of family letters, documents, pictures and especially Joe's prayer journals covering more than 50 years. Without access to these materials, there would be no book.

Larry Voyles for guiding me around the Harding University Library for a day of researching historical archives which finally surrendered documentation for much of the Cannon college era.

Geoff Ellis for kindly escorting me around Toronto to visit Joe's childhood neighborhood, including the church building where Joe broke a window with a rock. Also for arranging interviews with several of Joe's surviving friends.

Kathy (Cannon) Straker and husband Rick for their weekend visit to sort through Cannon family history, identifying people in pictures, and scouring a decade's worth of Joe's journals which saved me several research days.

Scott Ronyak and **Monica Lopez Taylor** for arduous hours transcribing audio interviews.

DeAnn Bennett, Donna Bates, Emily Vander Ark and **Jessica Bennett** for last-minute, long-hour, late-night (early-morning) editorial efforts to finalize my past-deadline manuscript!

Justin Vander Ark for scanning and editing old documents, pictures, and personalizing the maps of Japan, Okinawa, Papua New Guinea, and Ukraine.

Matt Taylor for investing dozens of artistic hours producing a graphite drawing of the front cover image of Joe.

Vicki Huffman for editorial expertise and friendly advice from front to back with this, our second book together.

Too Many Others to Name from the United States, Canada, Australia, Japan, Okinawa, Papua New Guinea, Indonesia, and Ukraine, who trusted me with their personal anecdotes of Joe and Rosa Belle. These yarns provided the necessary flair and flavor upon which every good story line depends.

CONTENTS

MAPS

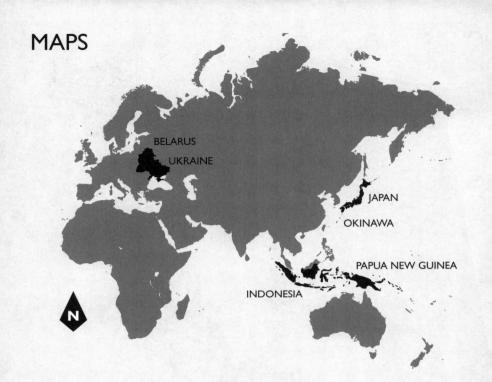

PAPUA NEW GUINEA

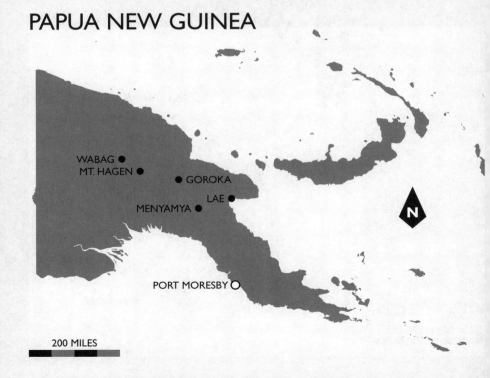

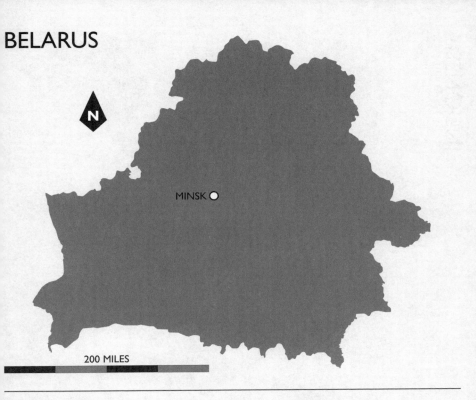

BELARUS

N

MINSK ○

200 MILES

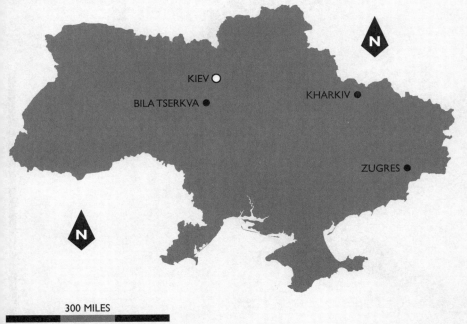

UKRAINE

N

KIEV ○

BILA TSERKVA ●

KHARKIV ●

ZUGRES ●

N

300 MILES

INDONESIA

JAYAPURA

JAKARTA

N

1000 MILES

FOREWORD

FOR MANY YEARS THE BRITISH produced two versions of select missionary biographies, one for adults, the other for children. Why? Among other purposes, they felt that by so doing they would plant seeds for missionaries in future generations. That proved to be true since many later missionaries recorded the impressions left on them by reading about Dr. Livingstone, William Carey, and others. Biographies may serve other purposes as well, but telling a true story about the life of "one who did it" still has the potential for inspiring, encouraging and even challenging the readers. David Sitton has done that in providing this readable account of the life and work of Joe Cannon.

For twenty years and more I have required my post-graduate students at Harding University to read an approved biography of a missionary as one of their assignments in the basic Global Evangelism course. Given the chance, I shall cheerfully add Sitton's book on Joe Cannon to that list.

Of course, there is also value in producing a critical but even-handed account of missionaries who made a lot of blunders. Most conscientious long-term missionaries I know want future workers to learn from them "how not to do it" as well as "how to do it" in comparable situations. Sitton's book is no effort at hagiography; he reports as well a few "warts" in Cannon's work. That makes him human, if an unusual human.

Those who will read this work will find that Sitton has provided a sensitive, appreciative but balanced account of a man who had a passion for people to know Christ. Sitton knew Joe first-hand for an extended period as a fellow worker in Papua New Guinea. That experience drove

Sitton to research and record a broader account of Cannon's dramatic personal life and indomitable work for his Master.

To those who had tidy organizational plans and pockets full of "tested strategies and methods" Joe Cannon was a bit of an irritant. In one of Joe's writings he was referring to those who were pushing methods used by the apostle Paul in the first century, often referred to as the "Pauline method." Joe quipped, "But I didn't marry Pauline; I married Rosa Belle." He had read books on missions but was prepared to depart from the recommendations when he entered new areas as different as Okinawa, Papua New Guinea, and Ukraine. Joe's flexibility, coupled with courageousness and all the accompanying risks, comes loudly through in Sitton's book.

Given knowledge of the best methods and insights carved out of past experience and current research, there is never a substitute for a life that embodies the message one preaches. Phillips Brooks famously defined preaching as "the communication of truth by man to man. It has in it two essential elements, truth and personality. Neither of those can it spare and still be preaching."[2] To understand Joe Cannon's work one must see something of the personality that embodied the message. Joe was smart, quick-witted, and at times very self-effacing, but no one who knew him would question his love for people and deep passion for them to know Christ. In addition to biblical affirmations about the "new birth" and "new creation," Joe knew existentially that Jesus Christ could and did change people's lives and make them useful. He was a living example of that.

I do not recall when I first heard of the Canadian fireball, Joe Cannon, but while working in England in the early 1960s I met an American military man who had known Joe in Japan and heard him debate a Buddhist priest. Long before I met Joe in the late 1970s I had heard from Harding University students how Joe had inspired them to do something meaningful with their lives. I knew him best during the time I taught in the M/1000 program in Memphis. In the following

---

2   Brooks, *Lectures on Preaching* (New York: E. P. Dutton & Company, 1898), 5.

20 plus years I had periodic contact with him until his death. He was unpretentious; he simply did what he concluded to be right and did it with vigor. May the memory of him, enhanced by this book by David Sitton, continue to produce fruit to the glory of God.

—C. Philip Slate, D. Miss
Missiologist, Author of *Lest We Forget:*
Mini-biographies of Missionaries of a Bygone Generation
Memphis, TN, 2014

PROLOGUE:
THE DREAM

Our hope is that ... we can preach the gospel in regions beyond you. For

we do not want to boast about work already done in another man's territory.[3]

JOE CANNON HAD A DREAM. It was first mentioned in a personal letter he wrote to a friend in 1950. "Dream" references are thereafter generously scattered throughout his 1960s journals. Allusions to the dream intensified in the 1970s, were listed more than 100 times during the 1980s, and escalated in their frequency throughout the 1990s and 2000s.

What was the dream? Joe didn't reveal it outright until later years and never described it fully. These private prayers were characterized by brevity: "Remember the dream, Lord." He often used incomplete sentences, once writing quaintly "our dream," as a line by itself on his prayer list. Nothing more was needed. The Lord understood.

But I didn't understand and couldn't figure it out. Only after I had pressed through 50 years of journals was it finally revealed. Of course, you must be "faithful to the end" of this book to learn the dream and perhaps become a part of its fulfillment.

For now I will say only, the accomplishment of Joe's dream will require wild men and women and spearheads.

---

3   2 Corinthians 10:15-16.

WILD MEN AND SPEARHEADS

I am out of my mind to talk like this . . .[4]

The gospel doesn't carry itself along its own merry way. When it runs, it runs on our legs. God's messengers are called upon to forcefully accelerate the gospel into hazardous situations, and front line soldiers for Christ are guaranteed to be busted up and bloodied in the fight. By definition, a "balanced" person will not do this. A more domesticated disciple will turn back when he deems it *unreasonable* to exchange leisure, physical safety, or financial security (much less his life) for the advancement of Christ.

Being something of a gospel wild man (or woman) is a necessary requisite[5] for a trailblazing pioneer to speedily spread *good news* or to be willing to die in the effort of spreading it. However, this was Joe and Rosa Belle's uncompromised missionary worldview. One might be a missionary without being crazy, I suppose. However, to be a gospel pioneer and a *leader* of gospel spearheads, along with other attributes, requires a sizable capacity to engage risk in ways that are viewed by most as irrational. Spearhead missionaries are those who view themselves as joyfully expendable for the advance of Jesus' name.[6]

Joe and RB actually *were* gospel spearheads. It is no embellishment to say that Joe gladly and recklessly[7] led with the crown of his own grey head into unreached regions for Christ—and he expected others to do the same. Perhaps more than any other missionary description, Joe esteemed the imagery of a spearhead. It is the metaphor of a *Hard Fighting Soldier* and the rationale for the title of his memoir. I've

---

4   2 Corinthians 11:23.

5   1 Corinthians 4:9-13; 2 Corinthians 4:7-12; 2 Corinthians 11:23-28.

6   Acts 20:24; Acts 21:13; Acts 15:26; Revelation 12:11.

7   Reckless / adjective: marked by lack of proper caution; careless of danger; utterly unconcerned about the consequences of some action.

trudged many miles with Joe, through the harshest territories in Papua New Guinea, and heard him sing and whistle as he walked:[8]

I'm a hard fighting soldier, I'm on the battlefield

I'm a hard fighting soldier, I'm on the battlefield

And I'm bringing souls to Jesus by the service that I yield.

I've got a helmet on my head, in my hand a sword and shield

I've got a helmet on my head, in my hand a sword and shield

And I'm bringing souls to Jesus by the service that I yield.

What a fellow fellowship, what a joy, sweet joy divine

What a fellow fellowship, what a joy, sweet joy divine

And I'm bringing souls to Jesus by the service that I yield.

He did it. He trained others to do it. And he did it until his final breath. Here is Joe's story.

---

8   *Hard Fighting Soldier*, author unknown. The third verse is one Joe made up as he huffed his way over a mountain ridge improvising with the words of a favorite hymn.

PART 1:
TANGLED ROOTS

JOE AND ROSA BELLE CANNON both had the surname *Cannon* at birth. Joe often said, "I'm a Cannon and I married a Cannon. We're a double-barreled family!"

The providential sharing of a surname tangles the roots of the couple's lineage. However, it also adds to the intrigue, as we see how the Lord later arranges Joe and Rosa Belle's (RB to family and friends) meeting in a college chapel service—a meeting which leads to romance, a quick marriage, and their departure as missionaries to Japan.

JOE CANNON LINEAGE

Joseph (Joe) Leonard Cannon was born into an English family in Philadelphia, Pennsylvania, on January 6, 1927.[9] Joe was named after his grandfather, Joseph Cannon, a British military officer[10] who became a casualty of the Second Boer War in South Africa.[11]

---

9   Details of Joe's early life were provided by Robin Cannon and Larry Voyles, Joe's youngest son and nephew respectively.

10   Joe told the family that his grandfather had been a member of the Coldstream Guard, an elite unit of the British Army. They were easily recognized by their tall bearskin hats.

11   1899-1902.

Apparently, grandfather Joseph had some association with the aristocracy,[12] but the specific connections are unclear. Before the war, Joseph married a "commoner" and was therefore ostracized by his family. Joseph and his wife had one son named Leonard before Joseph was killed in the war. The family banned Leonard's mother from having contact with her son, so Leonard was essentially orphaned at about nine years of age.

Following his father's death in the war, Leonard's unscrupulous uncles sold him to a farmer in Canada in order to get rid of him and collect on their brother's inheritance. They showed the child beautiful pictures of moose and told him fanciful stories of how wonderful life could be for him in Canada. Leonard was tricked into getting on a ship with other war orphans leaving England. His immigration, however, proved to be more like being sold into slavery as he did seven years of forced labor on a farm in Ontario.

As World War I began to escalate, Leonard, still wearing his short work pants, fled the farm to join the Canadian Army. Though big for his 16 years, he must have looked like a kid in shorts because he was turned away. Undeterred, Leonard ran back to the farm, "borrowed" a pair of long pants in order to appear older, and succeeded in being inducted into the army.

One reason Leonard enlisted in the army was to try to reconnect with his birth family in England. As a sergeant in the Canadian military, he used his off-duty time to show up unexpectedly at the family home. When Leonard revealed his identity to his uncles he was again soundly rejected. This time the excuse given was that he had no proof of identification. From that moment on, Leonard determined to make his own way in his new homeland.

Leonard finished four years in World War I. Fighting in the trenches of France, he was hit by shrapnel from a German potato-masher hand grenade and painfully rehabbed the final months of the war in a Canadian

---

12 People in the highest class of society, who usually have money, land and/or political power and who often have special titles, such as "duke", "duchess" or "countess."

hospital. He carried metal shards in his lower legs for the rest of his life. Joe recalled as a child trying to feel the shrapnel in his father's shins and calves.

Joe with older sister Aileen (1930)

Upon his return to Canada, Leonard married Ivy Nutter who had been born in Lancashire, England, and had also immigrated to Canada as a child. He often said he loved her so much because she was the only person who ever really cared for him. In the mid-1920s, Leonard and Ivy ventured south to Philadelphia, Pennsylvania, looking for work, which he found with an aluminum company. Philadelphia became Joe's birthplace in 1927, but by the early 1930s the family had returned to Canada.

[Joe's official nationality was playfully debated through the years, however, having been born in the United States he always enjoyed the full rights and privileges of American citizenship. When Joe turned 18 while at Harding College, he was forced to choose between Canadian and American citizenship. His selection of American citizenship became providentially useful during the six decades he served as a missionary for Christ.]

Large and rough-edged, Leonard was also not a particularly religious man. He ruled his family with a stern hand but didn't allow anyone else to interfere with his children. Once, when Joe and his friends had been in the railway yard stealing scrap metal, the security guards, known as *bulls*, went to the Cannon home to voice their complaint. Slow to listen and quick to throw a punch, Mr. Cannon knocked one of the guards out and chased them off his property.

His whole life, Leonard exhibited a fierce loyalty to king and country, even to the point of re-enlisting during World War II. He returned to

London during the Battle of Britain[13] and invested himself in digging survivors and corpses out of the rubble from German bombing raids.

Leonard and Ivy raised two children, Joseph Leonard and Aileen Boyce. Following Leonard's death in 1962, Joe and Rosa Belle brought his mother to live and work with them in the Orient. Ivy died in 1965 and is buried at the International Cemetery in Naha, Okinawa.

ROSA BELLE CANNON LINEAGE

Rosa Belle Cannon was born on November 19, 1922, to Earl Lamar and Ida Bell Cannon, hardworking, depression-era ranchers in Henryetta, Oklahoma.[14] Rosa Belle's grandfather, Thomas William Cannon, had meandered into the Indian Territory of Oklahoma from Texas during the Civil War and settled there.

Earl met and married Ida when he worked for his father who operated five cotton gins along the Canadian River in Oklahoma. At first the couple lived in a covered wagon and roamed the countryside as gin-saw sharpeners. However, following the tragic death of their first child at the hands of a drunken doctor, Earl worked at a drugstore and grocery in Stuart, Oklahoma, where Troy was born. Eventually Earl purchased a 40-acre farm in Henryetta where they settled permanently. It was here their other three children, Vanita, Pauline, and Rosa Belle, were born.

Rosa Belle's older sister Pauline recalls an incident when they were children of six and seven. The two girls found a large clump of ragweed near the old pig pen. They dragged it into the house and propped it up in a corner. Their mother allowed them to decorate their "Christmas tree" with paper chains and popcorn they had strung together with needles and thread.

---

13   The Battle of Britain was a fierce air campaign waged by the German Air Force against the U.K. during the summer and fall of 1940. The name of the battle comes from a notable speech by Prime Minister Winston Churchill in which he said, "The battle of France is over. I expect the battle of Britain is about to begin."

14   Rosa Belle's early life details supplied by Larry Voyles' extensive notes gathered from RB's older sister Pauline.

Teen-aged Rosa Belle

There usually wasn't much for Christmas, but Pauline remembers one particular surprise: "We woke up and found two dolls on the foot of our bed." Earl had acquired the dolls as prizes for trading with a local grocery store. Another time Pauline said, "Dad got us two child-sized rocking chairs. RB's was red and mine was wood color."

The Cannon girls made their own clothes and quilt tops from flour sacks. In those days, flour mills sometimes produced softer material sacks that were nicely printed so people would purchase their products for the bonus fabric. The three girls sewed their own dresses and underwear for Earl and Troy from the less abrasive fabrics. Rosa Belle's life on the farm with rugged conditions would prepare her for the tough first years of living in austere war-torn Japan better than some who had grown up in cities and enjoyed easier lives.

Earl and Troy farmed the land while Ida and the girls tended their large garden. The farm provided milk, butter, and eggs, as well as beef, pork, and poultry. They always had plenty to eat and to share with others. Ida probably gave away tons of okra, beans, potatoes, and blackberries through the years. In the winter they ate jar-canned fruits and vegetables they stored in a cellar. Occasionally they enjoyed canned carp. Family members recalled eating wild game and that "buffalo tasted a lot like tuna."

Another talent the Cannon women excelled in was the skill of tatting (like crocheting). Ida was a quiet and simple woman who finished only the third grade, but as she did her tatting she was able to read her Bible or talk with those around her. She lovingly taught Pauline and Rosa Belle how to create baby booties, specially decorated with beadwork and ribbons which they joyfully gave to the newborns in the area.

As World War II revved up with the Pearl Harbor strike in 1941, Earl temporarily moved the family to Wichita, Kansas, where they worked on behalf of the war effort. At 17, Rosa Belle got a job with Boeing Aircraft. Exceptionally smart, she was quickly made responsible for producing schematics that were used in assembly units. Pauline became a wiring inspector at Beech Aircraft, while Earl was in charge of building maintenance for the hangars where the planes were built.

With victory guaranteed for the Allied Forces on D-Day, June 6, 1944, Earl relocated most of the family back to their Henryetta homestead. However, Troy was drafted into the war effort, and Rosa Belle opted to stay in Wichita for another year to work and save money in preparation to attend Harding College. After all, college is not cheap. The enrollment fee was $10.00 for the art classes she planned to study! By the fall of 1946, Rosa Belle was able to enroll at Harding College.

Rosa Belle's father died in 1965 and her mother in 1973. Both are buried in Henryetta, Oklahoma. RB's brother, Troy, died in Searcy, Arkansas, in 1986, and her older sister, Vanita Cannon Mueller, passed away in North Carolina in 1988. At the time of this writing, Pauline Cannon Davis is the only surviving sibling. She still lives in Searcy.

RIDEAU RATS

As Rosa Belle was growing up on the Henryetta farm in the mid-1930s, Leonard Cannon (Joe's father) transferred his family back to Canada where Toronto became the place Joe knew as home. For the Leonard Cannon family, 18 Rideau

Reunion of the Rideau Rats at Camp Omagh: Bert Thompson, Keith Thompson (no relation), Murray Hammond, Warren Whitelaw and Joe Cannon (early 1990s)

Street became ground zero for the next decade. Like most young boys in Toronto, Joe eagerly spent as much time as he could skating and playing ice hockey and other winter sports.

Although Joe's father sent him to Western Technical High School to learn the trades, carpentry, drafting, and metal shop, Joe wasn't cut out for it. Robin, Joe's youngest son, told me, "Dad is about as technical as a brick. He didn't know the right end of a hammer for the rest of his life. And he didn't *want* to know."

Joe's disinterest in trade school stoked a curiosity in new recreations. He and some of his high school buddies[15] began looking for trouble, which was cleverly disguised as adventure. One of their favorite adventures was to find Catholic gangs in the nearby neighborhoods and beat them up. Joe became a fighter and the leader of the *Rideau Rats*,[16] a gang of local street thugs.

Toronto street gangs of the 1930s were nothing like modern inner-city violence. Bad stuff went on, but there wasn't the endemic prevalence of drugs, drinking, and drive-by viciousness that is common now. The Rideau Rats got into fights and stole cokes and candy from local grocers or iron from trains to sell to salvage dealers. But their only weapons were fists and feet.

One night, Joe's dad caught wind that the *Rats* were scheming to steal some iron at the train yard. Leonard went down to the yard, hid, and waited several hours. Then, sure enough, here came the *Rats*. When Joe pocketed a few iron scraps, Leonard burst out of hiding in a rage and shouted at Joe all the way home. In typical Joe fashion, he gave his son Robin the more explicit version of the story. "Dad kicked my backside all the way home until I finally crapped in my pants and had to crawl into the house and apologize to my mother."

As a low-level gambling bookie, Leonard had experienced enough of the streets to know he didn't want Joe going down that road. One afternoon Leonard arrived home from work on the streetcar earlier

---

15   Murray Hammond, Keith Thompson, and Brian Thompson among them.

16   Joe lived on Rideau Street, which is where the Rideau Rats moniker originated.

than usual. As he came toward the house, he saw a traveling salesman standing at his front door hustling his wares to Ivy. When the lecherous salesman tried to grab her and kiss her, Leonard lunged across the small front yard and pile-drove him through a plate glass window. He beat the man bloody and threw him onto the street, while Joe witnessed it all. This was the rough and tumble life for the Cannon family that shaped Joe's 13-year-old worldview.

Joe became the undisputed *Skipper* of the Rideau Rats which, some say, grew into a posse of more than 20 young men. They roamed their low-income neighborhood for about three years, instigating trouble wherever they went. However, the Rideau Rats began to unravel through a single rock-throwing incident.

About 1940, A.L. (Lynn) Whitelaw, a Church of Christ preacher, made it his habit to wander the streets looking to share the gospel with wayward kids. He began to take an interest in Joe and his errant friends. Brother Whitelaw repeatedly invited the boys to come to services at the Fern Avenue Church of Christ,[17] but the boys would have none of it. A.L. persisted with his evangelistic invitations, but the boys laughed, mocked him, and refused to go.

A.L. got the idea to invite the gang to play baseball on the church team. There actually was no team at the time, but the church members thought it might be a great time to start one. The congregation pooled their collections, bought team tee shirts and rounded up a coach from among the members. Sister Whitelaw baked a cake and the boys were lured off the streets, as Joe says, "with a little help from my fists."

One night, Joe took a notion to throw a rock through one of the church windows. Somehow Brother Whitelaw identified the culprits and cornered Joe. "OK, Joe," Brother Whitelaw said, "you have a choice

---

17   During my book research visit to Toronto in 2011, Geoff Ellis, a dear friend of Joe's for many years, generously toured the Rideau neighborhood with me. Joe's childhood house on Rideau Street and the building where the Fern Avenue Church of Christ congregated for many years have changed little. Joe's house is still a functioning residence. Sadly, the church building is now a Hindu Temple.

to make. You come to a series of Bible studies and I won't press charges for the broken window." Joe agreed.

But Brother Whitelaw wasn't finished. "Joe, we've got a church youth camp I want you to come to. It will be good for you. I'll pay for everything. You boys just come along and have a great time."

Joe was sure he didn't want to go to church camp! So A.L. employed another well-worn evangelistic strategy. "Joe, you know that church camp that I told you about? Did I mention that there would be a lot of girls there?" Suddenly, the young men were having second thoughts about "free food, a campfire, and lots of girls. . . ."

But the Rideau Rats weren't finished yet!

CAMP OMAGH

Omagh is the name of a small village in the vicinity of Milton, Ontario. In 1935, Mr. and Mrs. William B. Johnstone conceived the idea of inviting young people from the city to visit their farm for a few days of summer vacation. Part of the plan was also to provide good Christian fellowship for their own children.

The camp incorporated as the "Omagh Bible School" under the auspices of the Church of Christ in Canada and has continued until this day, providing young people with daily disciplines of worship, prayer, Bible study and lots of outdoor recreation. No doubt many hundreds, if not thousands, have come to believe in Christ through this Christian camp.

Due to the outbreak of World War II in 1939, Camp Omagh's attendance was slipping. By the summer of 1941, only 45 young people showed up. However, the 1941 session would prove to be incredibly impactful for many people, from many countries, in the decades to follow.

Because a week at Camp Omagh for the Rideau Rats was the punishment for breaking a church window, the ruffians arrived to serve their sentence (and meet the girls). However, Joe instigated so many mischievous stunts during his first 24 hours that he was locked in the boy's outhouse. Being the hellion he was, Joe lit a match and set the outhouse on fire—while he was still locked in it. Camp counselors rushed to put out the fire and let him out. As Joe recalled, "[The outhouse] was so nasty it deserved to be burned down!" [Setting fires seems to be a recurring theme for Joe, as we will see again, when he gets to Harding College, and a third time, as a missionary in Papua New Guinea 30 years later.]

Joe didn't make it one full day before he was expelled from Camp Omagh. However, due to gasoline rations during the war, no one had extra fuel to haul Joe back to Toronto. So he was allowed to stay. Meticulous Providence! By the end of the week, Joe and two of his friends, Murray Hammond and Bruce Sweezie, were profoundly converted to Christ through the gospel! Joe, Murray, and Bruce were baptized at Camp Omagh on July 10, 1941.[18]

The conversion of their leader became the demise of the *Rideau Rats*. Immediately upon his return to the city, Joe began going after his buddies with the gospel. He went to their houses on Sunday mornings and dragged them to the meetings. And he won some of them for Christ. Joe has said that over the years one of the old *Rats* went to prison, one became a Catholic priest, and a half-dozen of them became gospel preachers.[19]

Joe also aggressively sought ways to discuss the gospel with his parents, which often led to heated arguments. One time Joe asked, "Dad, would you just read the New Testament? I challenge you to just read it." Leonard was a hard-drinking kind of guy, but he loved his son and, evidently, began to read the Bible.

His mother Ivy came from a long ancestral line of superstition, spiritualism, and frequent interactions with spirit mediums.[20] Many Friday nights, his parents had attempted to communicate with their dead relatives. When Joe and his sister were young, sometimes they were fed and put to bed early. However, Joe crawled down the hallway to watch the festivities. Leonard and Ivy gathered around the dining

---

18   Wilma Johnstone Moore. "The Omagh Bible School: The Early Years" (booklet). Publishing date unknown.

19   Murray Hammond, Keith Thompson, and Bruce Sweezie among them.

20   This was told to me by Robin Cannon in a taped interview in Memphis, TN, in 2011.

table with one or two other people. They put a candle in the middle of the table, held hands and—usually led by his mom or one of Joe's aunts—tried to conjure up departed relatives. Joe poked his head around the corner of the wall so he could see if anyone showed up. He claimed that he saw objects move in unexplainable ways and heard strange, unrecognizable voices, even though he knew everyone in the room. Joe never understood these experiences but insisted they were real and very spooky.

This was his home environment as Joe was attending Western Technical High School and trying to give gospel witness to his parents. Even as a new believer, Joe was eager to preach the gospel wherever he could, sometimes going on weekend or summer-long gospel campaigns in northern Ontario.

When Joe returned home after one of those trips in 1942, he walked into the house and found his dad, mother, and sister Aileen sitting in chairs quietly grinning. They didn't even stand up to greet him with a hug. His dad announced, "Joe, I just want you to know that we have all believed in Christ. We're Christians!" Joe was jubilant! He told the story many times over the years, about how his family had come to faith in Christ during those happy days.

Two years later, as a new student at Harding College, Joe wrote in an essay that described his affection for the ministry of Camp Omagh: "Omagh is the dearest spot on earth to me . . . I hope I can also be of some use in bringing others into the Kingdom."

HARDING COLLEGE

Because of World War II, many young men were in a hurry to grow up. Joe quit Western Tech high school two years early, passed the college entrance exams and, at 15 years old, headed south to Searcy, Arkansas, to enroll at Harding College in the fall of 1942.

When the fresh flock of 1946 freshmen arrived on campus, Joe was eager to help (and meet) the incoming females. Joe made himself available around the Patty Cobb Dormitory Building where the ladies were to lodge. Evidently one of the new girls he assisted on the first day of the new school year was Rosa Belle Cannon.[21]

One of Joe's goals, he said somewhat jokingly, was to date every single girl on campus. He started working through the alphabet. When he got through the "A's" and "B's," he turned his attention to the girl seated next to him in chapel every day. The students were seated in alphabetical order so, naturally, the two Cannons sat side by side. One morning as Joe sat down next to Rosa Belle, he took notice of the Oklahoma farm girl with this brief journal entry: "Not bad looking." He never finished working his way through the alphabet as he realized his soul mate was sitting beside him every morning. They were engaged by December, married five months later, and left for the mission field in Japan eight months after that.

Joe's first job on campus was as a "sanitary-engineer"(janitor). His primary duty was to drive a donkey cart between the various buildings, collecting trash and hauling it to the dump. Joe named the campus mule "Napoleon" because of his "Boney Parts" and complained about his stubbornness. When Joe came around the ladies dormitories he would yell out a warning to them, "Man on 3rd floor." Then they knew to stay in their rooms if they were still in bathrobes and hair curlers.

Joe and the campus mule "Napoleon"

On one particularly cold morning, Joe lit an actual fire near Napoleon's rump to get him moving. As soon as he was able, Joe deserted the old mule and cart in favor of tutoring high school students. Joe's

---

21 Rosa Belle took her son Robin to the Patty Cobb Dormitory, where she had roomed as a freshman. At the front of the building she pointed to the third floor, third window from the left. "That's where Joe carried my things."

Harding College (1947)

friends remember that he had a joyful spirit even as he collected trash with a stubborn mule. He was always a cheerful guy and did not resent a chore others may have thought beneath them. Joe never avoided hard work.

Perpetual prankster that he was, Joe cut class on occasion. As the sanitary-engineer, he knew where all the hidden hallways, maintenance entryways, and ventilation spaces were. In one of his classes, the professor was a bit hard of hearing. Joe brought in a small alarm clock and set the alarm for 15 minutes before the end of class. The teacher, thinking he heard the school's bell, let everyone out of class early. Another trick was to report for class just long enough to get through roll call. When the teacher turned to write on the blackboard, Joe would crawl to the back of the classroom and escape through a hatch into a service exit.

Despite all his pranks and practical jokes, Joe's college accomplishments were numerous. He graduated in 1947 with a double major in Bible and History and minors in Speech and English. He was the president of the Lambda Sigma men's social club (1946-47), sang in the Harding Chorus, excelled as a member of the Debate Team, and managed the circulation of the *Petit Jean* (college annual). He also had several leading roles and a number of one-man acts as president of the Campus Players drama club, played football, and was an all-star pitcher for the intramural softball team. In addition, he preached frequently on and around campus.[22] Underneath his picture in the Harding Annual in 1947 was a suitable statement: "Nothing great was ever achieved without enthusiasm." Joe Cannon never lacked for energy, effort, or enthusiasm.

---

22   These accomplishments and more are listed in the Harding Annuals, 1944-47.

Rosa Belle was equally gifted but quiet, shy, and modest—the opposite of Joe's boisterous persona. Joe was actually a humble man; he was just brash about it. Rosa Belle was an excellent student, an accomplished artist, and nominated for Senior Queen. But most importantly, she was the level-headed balance that Joe needed to keep him on an even keel. Her genius was that she could bridle him without controlling him.

Rosa Belle, Harding College (1946)

Joe and Rosa Belle were missionaries for Christ, but they were unsure about a specific future location to serve Him. However, they agreed completely on two things: they wanted to direct their efforts to those places where the gospel was least known. Within that parameter was a second ambition—to reach out to the "poorest of the poor."

As Joe's and Rosa Belle's college days came to an end, clarity for their next steps came through a startling sequence of confirmations.

PART 2: JAPAN (1947-1961)

JAPAN'S JOLTING AIR ATTACK ON Pearl Harbor on December 7, 1941, catapulted the United States into the worldwide conflict. Joe was a fledgling chap of fourteen, finding his way around the streets of Toronto on that momentous morning, while Rosa Belle was a young woman of nineteen, living in rural Henryetta, Oklahoma.

By the time Joe arrived at Harding College, Japan was already intruding on his mind. His older sister, Aileen, had married a man named Zimmerman who was an aviator with the legendary Flying Tigers.[23] No doubt his larger-than-life tales of aerial firefights over the Pacific raised Joe's interest in Japan.

By the beginning of Joe's senior year in 1946, stories of the famous, beach-battering assaults at Normandy[24] and Iwo Jima[25] and the atomic

---

23   The Flying Tigers were made up of three squadrons of about 20 aircraft each. The fighter planes were easily recognizable by their colorfully painted, shark-faced nose cones. Their first war flights were on December 20, 1941, only 12 days after the bombing of Pearl Harbor. The Flying Tigers were extremely effective in aerial combat throughout the South Pacific and Europe. (Phone conversation with Joe's sister Aileen Boyce on June 25, 2013.)

24   June 6, 1944: 2,500 Americans died, along with 3,000 British and Canadian troops. www.history.navy.mil.

25   February 19, 1945: Iwo Jima was a 36-day battle in which 2,400 American fatalities were registered on the first day alone. A total of 6,891 American soldiers and 22,000 Japanese soldiers died in this single battle. www.iwojima.com.

bombs that decimated the Japanese cities of Hiroshima[26] and Nagasaki[27] were already dominating the nation's consciousness. National anxiety was palpable. College students, gripped by these historic world events, were understandably worried how it would affect their lives after graduation.

With the convergence of grim wartime realities, looming college responsibilities, and his increasing desire to carry the gospel to the neediest places on earth, Joe felt an unusual urgency. And, once more, Japan unexpectedly plunged itself deep into his heart—this time in a most improbable—but permanent—way.

MACARTHUR'S MISSIONARY CALL

The A-bomb obliteration of Hiroshima brought a swift and conclusive end to the war. More than 160 Japanese cities were reduced to rubble.[28] The war, at least for Japan, ended when Emperor Hirohito announced his nation's surrender during a radio broadcast.[29] The Great War was finally over for the rest of the world 17 days later with the belated surrender of Germany to France. On that same day, September 2, 1945, Japanese officials, with MacArthur by their side, signed an unconditional surrender on the deck of the USS Missouri in Tokyo Bay.

Japan's post-war morale was utterly crushed. The atomic bombs had unleashed an unprecedented brutality and devastation upon the war-torn country that plunged them into physical, emotional, and

---

26   August 6, 1945: Hiroshima had a population of 350,000 people. Two-thirds of the city was flattened: 70,000 people were killed immediately and 70,000 more died from radiation within five years. (*The Atomic Bombing of Hiroshima and Nagasaki* by Jennifer Rosenberg; www.history1900s.about.com).

27   August 9, 1945: Nagasaki was a city of 270,000 people; 70,000 died at impact or from injuries, including radiation, before the end of the year. (*The Atomic Bombing of Hiroshima and Nagasaki* by Jennifer Rosenberg).

28   Including Tokyo, Osaka, Yokohama, Kobe, Hiroshima and Nagasaki. Tim Shorreck, *The Red Flags over Tokyo*. Article reprint available at www.timshorreck.com.

29   August 15, 1945.

spiritual ruin. Improbably, MacArthur himself eagerly stepped into this demoralizing void and devised a comprehensive strategy for both the material and spiritual restoration of Japan.[30]

In November 1945, General MacArthur, a lifelong Episcopalian, assembled a delegation of American clergy at his headquarters in the Dai-Ichi Insurance Building in downtown Tokyo. Sensing the urgency to act expeditiously to fill the "spiritual vacuum" created by the cataclysmic war-ending events, he urged Christian leaders to immediately deploy 1,000 missionaries to Japan. "If you do not fill it with Christianity," he told them, "it will be filled with communism."[31]

The general categorically believed that an essential element in the successful reconstruction of Japanese society, as well as an antidote to communism, was a spiritual overhaul. Shortly before his death in 1964, MacArthur recalled that "the Japanese needed spiritual leadership as well as material administration. I had to be . . . a theologian of sorts."[32]

MacArthur's call to send missionaries into Japan became an often repeated, wide-reaching and very public appeal. He brashly lobbied a wide range of churches and Christian institutions to direct their assistance, especially missionaries, as quickly as possible toward Japan.[33] Interestingly, Harry R. Fox, Sr., of the Church of Christ, became the first post-war missionary allowed to return to Japan. He was sent by the War Department as an interpreter for the Atomic Bomb Casualty Commission.[34] Mr. Fox would soon become a good friend and mentoring colleague of Joe and Rosa Belle Cannon.

---

30   Lawrence S. Wittner, *MacArthur and the Missionaries: God and Man in Occupied Japan*, Pacific Historical Review 40, no. 1, (Feb. 1971).

31   Tim Shorreck, *The Red Flags over Tokyo*. Blog post. www.timshorreck.com.

32   Douglas MacArthur, *Reminiscences: General of the Army*, 322, 324 (1965).

33   MacArthur's incessant pleading is well documented. John Gunther, *The Riddle of MacArthur (1951); Kazuo Kawai, Japan's American Interlude* (1960); William P. Woodard. *Religion-State Relations in Japan. Contemporary Japan*, 640-676 (1957).

34   Kenny Joseph, *The Genesis of Post-War Christian Ministries in Japan*. (Date unconfirmed).

ORDERS FROM HEADQUARTERS

One of General MacArthur's fervent missionary pleas[35] was delivered at a chapel service in the fall of 1946. Dr. George Benson, President of Harding College and a former missionary to China himself, read the appeal which described the crucial need for a speedy deployment of gospel preaching missionaries to Japan.

JOE WAS INSTANTLY AND FIERCELY COMPELLED BY MACARTHUR'S DIRECTIVE!

Jim Elliot[36] famously said in regard to the so-called *missionary call*: "I don't need a vision, I have a verse!" Joe believed that his marching order was: "Go into all the world and preach the gospel to all creation."[37] When missionaries through the years asked him how to know *where* to go, he would say, "Open your bible, open a map, and pray to the Lord of the harvest. That's how you get your orders from headquarters." Joe was already moving toward cross-cultural mission during college. However, that morning in chapel he received his own specific assignment.

Within weeks, Joe made the seven-hour drive to Henryetta, Oklahoma, during Christmas break to seek permission from Earl Cannon to marry Rosa Belle. Evidently, Joe and RB were "somewhat engaged" while waiting for Earl's reply. Finally, on February 17, Joe received a brief but amiable handwritten go-ahead for wedlock.

---

35 I'm not sure if this particular plea was a letter or transcript from a radio speech. MacArthur's missionary appeals to Christian colleges were many. A subtle reference to this chapel announcement can be found in the Harding Library archives (*The Bison*, February 13, 1947). However, no actual copy of the elusive letter (or transcript) has yet been located. The best indication of its existence, perhaps, is Joe's own testimony about the morning he heard MacArthur's missionary call and was compelled into 60 plus years of missionary service.

36 One of the "Ecuador 5" who were slaughtered by the Waodani Indians of Ecuador on January 8, 1956.

37 Mark 16:15.

With permission secured, Joe officially proposed marriage[38] and asked her to go with him to Japan. Rosa Belle's enthusiastic "Yes!" was the first of countless occasions where she would affirm and follow Joe over the next 55 years of marriage and missionary globetrotting.

A DOUBLE-BARRELED CANNON

Joe and RB were married five months later, on May 20, 1947. Stoy Pate, a preacher for the Central Church of Christ, a small congregation in Shawnee, Oklahoma, officiated. Patsy Cannon recalls that a chandelier somehow came loose during the wedding vows and crashed loudly to the

Joe and Rosa Belle Wedding (May 20, 1947)

floor. Brother Pate deftly remarked that it was nothing to be concerned about as "that sort of thing happens whenever two cannons get together!" (Joe and RB were sometimes referred to as "the first and only double-barreled cannon.")

Following the wedding, Joe and Rosa Belle unwaveringly devoted their collective energy to carrying the gospel of God's Son to the Land of the Rising Sun.

General MacArthur's appeal for new recruits fueled an ongoing enthusiasm for Japan among the college students. The November 1947 Lectureships on Harding's campus turned into a virtual mission conference rallied around the theme of "Reaching Japan for Christ!"

---

38 Robin Cannon says that when he was a student at Harding, Rosa Belle took him to the spot on campus where Joe proposed. It was the Hendricks Building (now the Nursing Building). The door had been removed in remodeling, but the doorway was still there.

One conference speaker, O.D. Bixler[39], had already worked as a missionary in Japan until he was expelled from the country at the onset of World War II. He graphically described the countryside which lay in ruins after the relentless bombardment. Another speaker was a soon-to-be new missionary to Japan named E.W. McMillan. Brother McMillan had recently returned from an exploratory outing to see the post-war opportunities for himself and issued a passionate plea for new missionaries. Still another, an unnamed missionary, who had labored in the Philippines, stirred many with stories of his captivity in a Japanese prisoner of war (POW) camp. Several well-known Church of Christ ministers, such as Dr. Otis Gatewood and Dr. Clifton Ganus also spoke convincingly of the vast prospect for gospel advance in Japan.

As a result of these lectureships, a group of 16, including singles and married couples, began to meet each morning at 6 a.m. for a concentrated study of Japanese, using lingua-phone records, books, and language tutors. This eager band of missionary trainees also gathered for prayer each afternoon.[40] Out of this initial language study and prayer group, three young couples developed into a mission team determined to make an impression for Christ among the distressed peoples of post-war Japan.

SEA VOYAGE AND CULTURE TRAUMA

In December 1947, only seven months into their marriage, Joe and Rosa Belle left Toronto on their lengthy journey toward Japan. They were commissioned under the spiritual oversight of the Fern Avenue Church of Christ but enjoyed financial and prayer assistance from several churches in Canada and the United States.[41] Joe and RB

---

39   Orville Bixler and his wife first went to Japan in 1918, immediately following the conclusion of World War I. Logan J. Fox, *History of Mission Work in Japan*, an unpublished work, page 8.

40   Language study and prayer took place in Administration Building, room 109. *The Harding Bison*, Feb. 27, 1947.

41   The Bay View Church (Toronto), the Orient Street (Stamford, TX) and Sand Hill

joked that they would enjoy some private, honeymoon time on the Pacific "cruise" to Japan. But Virgil and Lou Lawyer and Charlie and Norma Doyle, two of the young couples from Harding College, journeyed with them. To lower expenses the three wives shared one cabin, while their husbands occupied another. Not quite the honeymoon that Joe and RB anticipated!

RB on board the USS General Gordon (January 3, 1948)

The three couples boarded an old steamship, the USS General Gordon,[42] in San Francisco on January 3, 1948. Lou Lawyer remembers the voyage well since both she and Joe celebrated their 21st birthdays somewhere in the middle of the Pacific Ocean. They arrived in Yokohama, Japan, two weeks later on January 16. Orville Bixler, whose first wife had died a short time before, collected the new missionaries at portside and took them directly to her memorial service.

Lou Lawyer remembers Brother Bixler as a wheeler-dealer, but in the good sense that meant he was able to get things done. He frequently purchased supplies from the Army Surplus and sold them to the missionaries, including dented, unlabeled tinned foods and flour which was often specially "flavored" with weevils.

---

congregations (Newport, AR) supported the Cannons for 60, 49, and 60 years respectively. The Highland Church (Memphis, TN) lovingly cared for Joe and RB in later life until their deaths—a stellar partnership of more than 40 years.

42   The USS General Gordon was built in 1885 and launched her maiden voyage on April 20. The Gordon was converted into a military transport ship that served the U.S. Navy in World War II. While in civilian service, she made numerous calls at Shanghai, China, and is believed to be the last American ship to leave that port before the Communist takeover in 1949. The Gordon was modernized in 1953 and spent several years escorting troops back and forth across the Atlantic. She served briefly during the Korean War and on limited missions in Viet Nam in 1967. The General W. H. Gordon's final decommissioning occurred when she was stricken from the Naval Vessel Register in 1986 and sold for scrap in April 1987.

Bixler also arranged to rent a vacant house, one of the few that was not a heap of rubble from the war. The house had several sparsely furnished bedrooms where the greenhorn missionaries would settle in and get oriented to their gloomy surroundings.

Japan in January was bitterly cold. It was arranged for a Japanese woman named Kinezawa to be their language trainer. Every morning, the group bundled up in the frosty shack and buckled down for linguistic and culture study. Rosa Belle was by far the best language learner among them, possibly because her childhood friends had been Creek (Muskogee) Indians, and she had some experience speaking their tribal tongue. Lou Lawyer's memory of these tutoring sessions was not pleasant. The first sentence she wanted to learn was, "Hey, sir, may I inquire? Is there a secondhand bookstore in the area?"

Achieving foreign language fluency is always intimidating, and Japanese is a particularly formidable antagonist. The team's early efforts to compose coherent phrases came out as awkward garbling. Early on, Virgil Lawyer was met with puzzled faces when he spoke of the Jews and Gentiles. He mistakenly called them Jews and "hot water bottles."

It was no surprise to those who knew him that Joe was apparently a bit loose with the language. His most winsome quality in linguistic acquisition was an absolute fearlessness to give it a try, anywhere, anytime. Joe was eager to preach! Just a couple of minutes into his first attempt, a local listener interrupted him with a startling question. "Who is this great *turtle* of whom you speak?" Evidently, the word for "turtle" is "kam*e*" while the word for "God" is "kam*i*." Undeterred, Joe simply apologized for the error and plunged back into his text.

Joe may not have always been linguistically accurate, but he was never afraid to put his mouth where his heart was for the gospel. Joe and Rosa Belle eventually became beautifully fluent in Japanese. Joe also learned the alphabets of Hiragana and Katakana and became proficient in reading Kanji.

More than 30 years later, in Papua New Guinea, Joe and RB would often be heard rattling off Japanese to each other when they didn't want others to understand them. It was amusing how RB could get his immediate attention with a well-chosen phrase or two!

After the team spent three freezing, frustrating months with a language tutor in Tokyo, Brother Bixler relocated them to Omika, 100 miles away on the northeastern coast. E.W. McMillan had recently started a small Bible school nearby. Virgil and Lou Lawyer rented a small Japanese-style house, while the Doyles and Cannons shared a kindergarten building that had been converted into a house in the community of Taga, one train stop north of Omika.

A comparison of the personality types of the six individuals within the three-couple team is intriguing. Virgil Lawyer was a congenial, go-along-to-get-along leader who was able to work well with Joe, the sharp end of the stick: a vocal, visionary, trailblazing spearhead. Lou Lawyer had a temperament that tended to see everything in black and white, but apparently was mentally tough and persevering. Lou Lawyer and Norma Doyle were admitted germaphobes, which can be awkward for missionaries who often serve in areas not known for hygienic conditions. Rosa Belle was physically and spiritually durable and was more accustomed than some to ever-changing circumstances, especially uncomfortable living conditions. RB was also a good mediator and was adept at decelerating Joe to a manageable hustle.

All six members of the team were spiritually strong and persistent in their pledge to advance the cause of Christ to the Japanese people. Without the indispensable spiritual guts and team loyalty they each possessed, they never would have overcome the obstacles to get to Japan, much less to endure those difficult first years. Lou Lawyer recalls, "We had some great times. We were like family, and like family, we sometimes had 'words.'" Team relationships were not without controversy. Lou and Joe, especially, had their quarrels, but she was also known to defend him aggressively if anyone else said anything negative about him.

Joe was the undoubted leader of the pack, an alpha-male[43], one of many in a long line of robust, agenda-setting, pioneering missionaries before him. Unlike the Lawyer and Doyle families, Joe required very little assistance from the older missionaries and was more than willing to go it alone and learn things the hard way.[44] But *going it alone* for Joe meant going it with Rosa Belle. Lou rightly observed, "Joe would not have made it without RB. He didn't care about his living conditions or even what he would eat. RB took care of him. She was a great mission-ary wife, able to ignore inconveniences and adapt to varying situations with grace. I loved and respected her greatly."[45] As sure of himself as Joe seemed to be, Lou pointed out, he was a remarkably flexible and incredibly compassionate person.

A legendary mischief-maker, Joe earned the title that the Japanese gave him: *Chami San* which means "clown." He once teased an older American missionary woman who always bowed in respectful Japanese fashion whenever she greeted him. Joe bowed lower than her, which caused the woman to bow even lower. Then he bowed lower still, until they were both bent over double. Joe kept a straight face as he con-tinued the charade for some time. Understandably, missionaries were sometimes annoyed by his antics. However, Joe's jovial good humor endeared him to the local people everywhere he went.

As a youngster growing up in Toronto, Joe had learned to play the accordion and harmonica and performed whenever a group gathered round. Even though he didn't have real bagpipes, he sometimes imi-tated them, holding his nose and replicating the sound by tapping his other hand against his throat. Joe carried his comedic performance all the way to remote regions in Papua New Guinea playing his faux bagpipes for grass-skirted villagers who had never seen a white man,

---

43   One who behaves in a very confident and/or intimidating manner.

44   Joe's favorite quip to me during my years with him in PNG, usually in response to my own strong-headedness in a situation was: "Go ahead! Any lesson worth learning, is worth learning the hard way!"

45   Larry Voyles' family history notes.

much less heard of a bagpipe. He caused quite a stir with his garish facial expressions as he played with and chased children—and sometimes even tribal chiefs—around the campfire, causing both shrieks of laughter and screams of terror. More often than not though, Joe's playfulness was a useful ice-breaker that transcended language and nearly insurmountable cultural differences, made quick friends, and fast-tracked late night dialog toward the gospel.

Don Brown relates a favorite Joe Cannon recollection from those early days in Japan. Joe curiously observed the difficult task that local men had in getting their feisty pigs to market on their bicycles. They would get the pigs drunk on *saki* until they passed out. Then they strapped them on their bikes and pedaled like crazy to get to market before the pigs sobered up. An angry, hung-over pig tied to a bicycle could be an unwelcome road hazard!

FOLLOWING CHRIST INTO THE CAVES

While in college, Joe and RB agreed they would go to the place of greatest need for Christ. The Lord guided them to Japan. Likewise, they decided to concentrate their best efforts on reaching the poorest of the poor. Quoting Joe, "I believed Jesus wanted me to

Post-war Japanese families were forced to live in caves

serve among the most unloved people I could find. At that time, the most unloved people were Japanese."[46]

Once the team transferred north during the latter part of 1950, they situated themselves in the Hitachi industrial complex, which had been a primary bombing target during the war. Near the community of Omika, Joe stumbled upon an interrelated series of caves[47] that had been dug into the rock hillside and which included more than 20 displaced families, still living in these hand-hewn holes in the ground. These caves had served as a bomb shelter for people whose homes were destroyed during the Allied attacks. Even five years post-war, Japan's economic infrastructure staggered along in virtual ruins. Joe lamented:

> Caves! Caves in the earth where fellow-humans dwell. Heatless, waterless, dark, damp, stinking holes in the dirt where the poorest of the poor live, neglected, despised and hopeless. As my heart stands transfixed by the sight, Scripture after Scripture reverberates through my soul. "Did I not weep for him that was in trouble? Was my soul not grieved for the poor?" The words of my Lord are heard, "I was a stranger and you took me in." And again, "Go and sell all that thou hast and give it to the poor." Yes, and that striking parable that begins, "There was a certain beggar named Lazarus . . ."
>
> How can I pass by day by day and withhold my hand from the poor? Brethren, how far shall we follow Jesus? Hear him, "The Spirit of the Lord is upon me, because he hath anointed me to preach the gospel to the poor." "He hath scattered abroad, he hath given to the poor." – The answer is plain, we must follow him into the caves![48]

Appalling cave conditions, combined with utter spiritual disorientation, compelled the team to initiate evangelistic efforts among the despondent cave-dwellers. Eventually, Joe supervised a far-

---

47   Joe referenced at least two locations (same area but different hillsides). Joseph L. Cannon, "The Poor Are Remembered," undated article, early 1950s.

48   This excerpt is from an age-yellowed, hand-corrected, typewritten article (undated, early 1950s). Joseph L. Cannon, " . . . we should remember the poor" Galatians 2:10. This is an early version of his article, "The Poor Are Remembered."

reaching fundraising effort, primarily among indigenous Japanese believers, Rotarians, local businessmen, community people, even elementary and high school students, to assist in the purchase of land and the construction of duplex housing for the indigent cavern community. He solicited financial aid from Canadian and American churches as well, but it seems the largest portion of the money was gathered locally.

As vital as it was to care for the destitute, the essential object of missions Joe would often say is: "Starting churches, left and right, day and night." When asked about the source for his lyrical quip, he simply said, "I'm quoting myself!"[49]

Joe didn't only speak poetically about church planting, he cared deeply and charged hard after the evangelization of the cave dwellers:

> [We] have taken the gospel to the destitute in these [caves] and the question of [the Apostle] James has been answered in the affirmative as the gospel has been received, "Hath not God chosen the poor of this world rich in faith, and heirs of the Kingdom which he hath promised to them that love him?"

> . . . A church meets in the caves of Izumigawa in the city of Hitachi . . . Altogether there are twenty families living in these caves. We are already preaching the gospel to them, but we must also help them in their physical plight. For the sum of $200 dollars each, twenty dwellings can be erected, totaling $4,000. Compared with what we spend on houses in North America, this is a paltry sum. Brothers Oka, Watanabe and I are "spearheading"[50] this project to the glorification of God.

---

49 From conversation notes: Larry Voyles and Joe Cannon.

50 A favorite metaphor was that of a spearhead; the first part of the spear that punctures a target. Joe's earliest use of this metaphor, that I can find, is this one in reference to the cave people.

"He that hath mercy on the poor, happy is he. O let not the oppressed return ashamed; let the poor and needy praise thy name." [51]

One humorous episode occurred in the mid-1950s when Joe rounded up an old station wagon to assist in the burial of one of the cave residents. He bundled up the corpse and slid it into the back of the car, presumably with the family in a car following behind. The roads in those days were horrible and Joe usually drove at a fairly rapid pace. Regrettably, the back door popped open and the blanket-bound corpse soared out the back bouncing along the road! Joe quickly stopped and, while directing traffic, retrieved his cargo and slowly proceeded to the cemetery. [52]

Monument of appreciation to the missionaries

By July 1956, a small congregation was established in the caves, and by March 1957, the duplexes were finished and joyfully celebrated. The cave Christians erected a modest memorial in honor of the missionaries and local leaders who had launched the relief effort. Engraved on one side of the rock monument, facing the road, was this declaration: "We are most grateful to the Lord through the name of Jesus Christ!" On the backside of the tribute, facing the Pacific Ocean was etched this heartfelt inscription, "By the grace of God and love by Christian brothers and sisters, we have been able to get out of our lives in the caves and move into real houses. In memory of this fact, we built this monument in March, 1958."

51 Joseph L. Cannon, "The Poor Are Remembered," " . . . we should remember the poor" Galatians 2:10.

52 Joe howled with laughter as he told the story to his son Robin while on a gospel bush patrol years later in Papua New Guinea. Robin related the story to me during an April 25, 2014 interview.

Because of my own curiosity about this part of Joe's ministry in Japan, I wanted to pinpoint the exact spot of the memorial. Lots of people seemed to know about it, but because of city expansion over more than five decades, no one recalled precisely where it was located. Someone directed me to Steve and Marcia Hasbrouck who were missionaries long ago with Joe and Rosa Belle. Marcia contacted her Japanese friend, Miyoko Kawakami, who shared my interest. Miyoko tried to discover the whereabouts of the caves and the elusive statue.

The caves were not difficult to track down. They are situated on the seafront between Taga and Hitachi on Rt. 245, precisely at the place where the Aukawa River flows into the Pacific Ocean, on the right bank. However, the monument itself was not found. Miyoko's friend Mitsugu Doi, one of Joe's earliest converts, believed he could pinpoint the caverns and historical memorial. Mitsugu Doi recalled that the plaque was only about one foot tall. Sadly, due to the reconstruction of Rt. 245 and a nearby bridge which was a landmark for locating the site, they found that the memorial stone apparently no longer exists.

Disappointed, but not deterred, Miyoko and Mitsugu Doi drove to a place marked by a distinctive cluster of cedar trees, known to be the place of the housing site. Once again, they found nothing except trees. Apparently the duplexes were at some point bulldozed as new homes were constructed, thus erasing this part of the history. Only the caves remain, mostly camouflaged by grassy overgrowth and a busy highway.[53]

JAPANESE RECEPTIVITY

Japan has been historically and profoundly opposed to the gospel of Christ. In a missionary newsletter, entitled "Frontiers of Faith,"[54] Joe briefly recited the history of this resistance.

---

53   I am indebted to Marcia Hasbrouck, Miyoko Kawakami, and Doi-San for their efforts to locate the caves, memorial monument, and the 20 houses that were built for the cave people.

54   Joe Cannon, "Frontiers of Faith" (circa 1951). This appears to be a newsletter that evolved into an article which Joe used for greater circulation.

In the year A.D. 736, a Nestorian missionary left China and came to Japan to preach the gospel. There is no record of the work that was done, and only one statement in ancient Japanese records indicating this event.

Francis Xavier met a young Japanese man by the name of Yajiro while doing mission work for the Catholic Church in India. He was so impressed by the zeal of this young man that he decided to come to Japan, and did so in 1549. After preaching two years, and receiving a great following, he returned to Europe. During a series of persecutions inflicted by the Feudal Era (1603-1868) of the Tokugawa, the work done by Xavier and the Roman Catholics was completely wiped out. The country was closed off to foreigners, and for 300 years Japan was cut off from the world.

The year 1859 brought Protestant missionaries from America to Japan. Four men, Williams, Hepburn, Verbeck, and Brown opened the way to the preaching of the Word of God. As Japan began to learn Western culture, the anti-foreign feeling diminished, and many missionaries from various denominations entered the country. Even so, their work was uphill, and progress was very slow. The Japanese were so rooted in tradition and Emperor Worship that their hearts were in no condition to receive the truth. Eventually, Church of Christ missionaries also entered Japan, beginning with brother McCaleb,[55] who spent many years before the war laboring here. They, too, faced many difficulties and hindrances to the progress of the gospel.

Here's a strategic question with an amazing, providential reply. How did the brutal atomic bomb drops at the close of World War II affect a tactical advantage for the advance of the Christian faith in Japan?

During the 1920s, the spirit of Japanese nationalism increased, until "through one incident after another, during the 1930s, Japan expanded its influence into Korea, Manchuria, and China until she felt capable of

---

55   J.M. McCaleb went to Japan in 1892 and worked there just short of 50 years. Two single missionaries, Sarah Andrews and Lily Cypert, remained in Japan throughout the war years, insisting that "Japan is our home." Philip Slate, email, August 2, 2014.

ruling over all of Asia."[56] Japan's furious disgust for the gospel persisted until the catastrophic conclusion of World War II.

Japan's pre-war audacity was predicated upon a belief that they were militarily invincible and destined to rule the world. Emperor Hirohito was not only the commander of the Japanese military, but he was also the High Priest of Shinto, and was believed by the people to derive his spiritual authority from ancestors who had ascended to become gods.

General Douglas MacArthur summarized the interwoven symmetry of the Shinto religion and Japanese feelings of imperialistic superiority, which had exacerbated Japanese resistance to the gospel for centuries:

> The Japanese people were told that the Emperor was divine himself and that the highest purpose of every subject's life was death in his service. The militarists who had led Japan into war had used this religion to further their efforts, and the state still subsidized it.

> During the progress of the war, these millions (of Japanese) heard of nothing but Japanese victories . . . With the sudden, concentrated shock of total defeat; their whole world crumbled. It was not merely the overthrow of their military might–it was a collapse of a faith, it was the disintegration of everything they had believed in and lived by and fought for. It left a complete vacuum, morally, mentally and physically . . . The falseness of their former teachings, the failure of their former leadership, and the tragedy of their past faith were all infallibly demonstrated . . .[57]

On New Year's Day 1946, the emperor issued a statement of unconditional surrender, which included a public renunciation of his

---

56   Logan J. Fox, "History of Mission Work in Japan," unpublished article, page 14.

57   Douglas MacArthur, *Reminiscences* (1964), McGraw Hill Book Company, pages 310-311.

own divinity, thus affirming his humanity. The emperor's translated statement read:

> We stand by the people and we wish always to share with them in their moments of joys and sorrows. The ties between us and our people have always stood upon mutual trust and affection. They do not depend upon mere legends and myths. *They are not predicated on the false conception that the Emperor is divine and that the Japanese people are superior to other races and fated to rule the world.*[58] (Author's italics)

The emperor's declaration that he was not deity was an unprecedented pronouncement that caused a spiritual revolution that "almost overnight tore asunder a theory and practice of life built upon 2,000 years of history and tradition and legend."[59]

A significant, post-war historical detail is that General MacArthur was established as the Supreme Commander for the Allied Powers (SCAP), which gave him acting authority over the emperor himself. Consequently, a crucial part of MacArthur's ongoing responsibility as military governor was to oversee Japan's material and spiritual reconstruction. MacArthur's strategy for combatting the false ideologies of Shintoism, Buddhism, and Confucianism was to infiltrate Japanese society with a substantial promotion and proclamation of the Christian religion.

One of the ways MacArthur sought to spread Christianity was to distribute Bibles throughout Japan. In one instance, the general sent a telegram to the Pocket Testament League (PTL) requesting Bibles. A telegram reply to MacArthur said, "We can print a million Gospels of John." MacArthur replied, "Make it ten million!" PTL supporters graciously responded with 11 million Gospels of John.[60]

---

58   Ibid, page 310.

59   Ibid, page 311.

60   www.ptl.org/museum/museumpix/decade1940's/macarthur_letter.html. Following the distribution of 11 million Gospels of John, MacArthur wrote this letter

MacArthur also sent a similar telegram invitation to the Gideon's International in 1949[61] asking for an organization representative to "make a first-hand survey of the situation" in regard to New Testament distribution. MacArthur concluded one correspondence with the Gideons by saying, "I assure you of my deep appreciation of your interest in the spiritual rehabilitation of the Japanese people."

As noted earlier, MacArthur repeatedly summoned stateside churches and Christian colleges to send a massive influx of missionaries who could provide a full spectrum of secular and spiritual education to facilitate the vigorous and rapid recovery of Japan.

In response to these post-war realities, Joe Cannon continued in his brief overview of Japan's spiritually impervious history by writing:

> Now, in the year of 1951, many of the difficulties have been removed. The past war has had a great effect upon Japanese life. Many hearts are now searching for the truth. The frontier has been opened up, and the way is clear for more pioneering work to be done . . . virgin soil here is waiting to be tilled . . . that will bring forth abundant crops if only pioneers will come . . .

> While nations are sending thousands to fight and die to hold the fortress of democracy in Korea, will not the Church send a few to enlarge the foothold being held against Satan's kingdom in Japan? Or shall we say, because of war scares, it's too risky to send workers to Japan? Is the American government saying, it's too risky to send men and equipment to Korea? While Americans are fighting for a material cause, are there not men and women willing to dare for the purpose of the gospel? Are there those who are dodging the call of God to occupy the

(December 8, 1949) of thanks and endorsement of the Pocket Testament League (PTL), www.ptl.org/museum/museumpix/decade1940's/macarthur_letter.html.

61 blog.gideons.org/2011/12/gideon-bibles-pearl-harbor.

ramparts of his Kingdom? So what, if war comes and sweeps away the lives of missionaries and money invested into Japan, have we not preached that faith will ride through the storms and that God will have victory at last? What's wrong with the brethren that they will refuse to send a missionary to Japan because of the war in Korea? Brother and Sister Max Mowrer[62] have been trying to get to Japan for the past year, and there are few to help them. Brother Mowrer is a fine preacher, [of] good reputation and worthy of support, but some are thinking more about the dollar than they are of God. . . .

Japan today is a frontier of faith. I recently visited a town in Ibaraki. I was told that I was the first foreigner to come to that place . . . very interesting, but more interesting was the fact the gospel has never been preached there. No! Not from the beginning of the world. But this is not an unusual thing. We are establishing churches in many places like this. Places where no worker (of any denomination) has worked. Truly we can say that we are "not building on another man's foundation." This is a pioneer work and a challenge to all those who want to pioneer for Christ. Come to Japan![63]

These slightly abbreviated paragraphs underline Japan's historical hostility toward the gospel, but also how the traumatic conclusion of World War II forged a *temporary* receptivity[64] of the Japanese populace

---

62 I include this personalized reference because it is classic Joe Cannon. I venture to say that he publicly, probably thousands of times in print and from pulpits, sought to assist new missionaries who were struggling for financial support. And he supported many of them himself. He put money into my own hands more than once!

63 Joe Cannon, *Frontiers of Faith*, (1951).

64 I leave it to missiologists familiar with the ongoing history of Christian mission in Japan to assess how long this gospel openness continued. "Receptivity" is a subjective thing. In a place where fierce antagonism has endured for centuries, even a brief respite feels friendly.

that enabled 1950s missionaries to advance the gospel among a genera-tion (partial generation, at least) of Japanese war-survivors.

The final two paragraphs of the quotation are also included for a nec-essary biographical purpose. Joe's vigorous tirade, pleading for gospel laborers, was not hollow rhetoric. Sizzling exhortations for believers to engage the Great Commission was the incessant throb of Joe's heart for the least-reached peoples that went on uninterrupted for more than 60 years.

POST-WAR MISSION STRATEGY: SCHOOLS

When life is good, spiritual health is not usually the uppermost felt need of a nation. In fact, affluence and leisure more often breed spiritual apathy than health. But when the personal or collective spiri-tual equilibrium of a nation is disrupted, then the everyday ethos of a people will, some-times, veer straight toward a spiritual reboot.

Teaching the gospel in schools

The immediate post-war impact for Japan reduced the nation to physical and fiscal rubble. But, even more, the ongoing reverberations of abject emotional and spiritual disorientation of the masses ignited a historic cultural craving for "good news." This was the spiritual vacuum that General MacArthur recognized and sought to remedy with the recruitment of godly men proclaiming the gospel.

Similarly, Japanese leaders of the late 1940s interpreted their cul-tural void as a dearth of education. They eagerly pursued both secular teaching and spiritual guidance as vital components in their country's reconstruction efforts. Because of the Japanese people's insatiable thirst for knowledge and education, even in the midst of physical and spiritual upheaval, schools became a desirable conduit for the spread of the gospel in the post-war turbulence. Schools were open and the missionaries stepped in!

GLORY DAYS

Missionary transportation

Over the next decade until about 1961, there was a noteworthy influx of additional missionary manpower and a wonderful flurry of social and gospel development along the northeastern coast of Japan. Joe referred to this era as the "glory days for the gospel." This may have been the happiest 12-year stretch of his missionary life. It was certainly the most fruitful period in the history of Church of Christ mission work in Japan.

As the gospel radiated out of Omika, many parts of Japan were influenced. From 1948 to 1956, Church of Christ congregations had grown from four to thirty-three, with an average of about four new church plants per year. The missionary team quickly grew to more than 40 missionaries spread out mostly along the eastern seaboard, north and south of Tokyo. The team vigorously, in every imaginable way, advanced the gospel.

IBARAKI CHRISTIAN COLLEGE

Because the missionaries were fully committed to using schools as a way to propagate the gospel, a Bible study in Ibaraki quickly developed into an informal Bible school. Within one year under the direct influence of four missionaries,[65] the Bible study evolved into the Ibaraki Christian College (ICC).[66] In rapid succession, both a high school and

---

65   Joe Cannon, Logan Fox, Virgil Lawyer, Charles Doyle, and E.W. Mcmillan should also be noted as significant in the founding of Ibaraki Christian College (ICC). *History of Mission Work in Japan*, page 16.

66   The first name of the school was *Shion Gakuen*.

Ibaraki Christian College, 11th graduating class. Joe and RB, front row, far right (1961)

college department were developed. O.D. Bixler rendered invaluable practical service in those early days, enabling ICC's success. Bixler also functioned as the first chairman of the ICC Board of Trustees.[67]

Ibaraki Christian College began with 60 students and a fiery opening ceremony speech by E.W. McMillan. It was an incredibly ambitious undertaking which required the help of three missionaries (Cannon, Lawyer, and Doyle), along with three full-time and five part-time Japanese teachers. One of Joe's classic letters[68] home may have included his greatest understatement: "In all, I teach 26 hours of Bible classes a week, which is a full load!"

Joe was only twenty-three years old at this time. Even though he had his B.A. degree from Harding College and was quickly gaining valuable experience, he was still a fresh-faced young missionary. He was tall (6 feet, 2 inches), lanky (150 pounds) and had thick, dark hair that naturally fell in uneven waves from side to side across his head. Not long after the commencement of ICC, a young man Joe had been teaching arrived

---

67   The initial ICC board of directors included four Japanese brothers who served in areas of primary leadership. They were Kaoru Takizawa-san, Shoichi Oka-san, Ryhachi Shigekuni-sa, and Masaichi Kikuchi-san. *Articles of Incorporation, Ibaraki Christian College*, 1948-49.

68   May 7, 1951. This information was passed along to me from Myrna Perry through Ruth Zimmerman.

one morning sporting a permanent wave hairdo acquired from a local beauty shop. When Joe asked him why he had done such a silly-looking thing, the young Japanese man replied, "Well, you have one!"

Clifton Ganus[69] recalls having a tough-to-eat meal with Joe. It was *suki-yaki* cooked wok style in soy sauce and served with a raw egg broken over the top. Cliff asked Joe, "Do you like that stuff?" Joe replied, "No, but I learned to eat it." As if to demonstrate, he quickly swallowed the bowl's contents. Another missionary at the same table poured his egg into the hot soy sauce to at least cook it slightly. With relief Brother Ganus copied the other missionary's way of dealing with the food. Cliff also tells of being offered raw fish and other unidentified delicacies which Joe always graciously accepted and ate with his Japanese friends.

By the mid-1950s, Ibaraki Christian College had become a two-year, four-semester fully accredited Christian College, offering a full catalog of theological and practical field courses. In addition to being a college, ICC expanded to include a kindergarten, elementary, junior high, and high school. Ninety-nine percent of all students who entered these various levels of education were non-Christians. Many students wanted to attend because of ICC's accreditation and the fact that it had one of the finest English language laboratories in the country.[70]

The student enrollment continued to increase to more than 1,400 students in the late 1950s. A campus report circa 1965 noted that more than 1,000 students were refused entrance due to lack of classroom space and a shortage of qualified teachers. The facilities expanded until 1969 when enrollment surpassed 1,800 students. Joe remarked that the entirety of the ICC educational ministry had become the "greatest single opportunity for reaching souls with the gospel in the entire Far East."[71]

Amazingly, ICC survived financially by collecting, in addition to meager student tuition, $5 per month student scholarships. Five dollars each month could keep one student in college and under daily gospel teaching!

---

69   Dr. Clifton L. Ganus II, age 89, was still Chancellor of Harding College in 2012.

70   Jack Bates, *The Work of Ibaraki Christian College*, Firm Foundation, December 14, 1965.

71   *Ibaraki Christian Educator, Vol XIX, No. 4, July-August,* 1969.

ICC's growth spurt lasted at least until 1992 when Joe returned to the campus and spoke to a combined chapel of 3,800 students.[72] Joe once summarized the impact of ICC, by saying, " . . . students receive daily Bible instruction, and engage in daily chapel worship and special prayer meetings. Through the Spirit of Christ, students coming from Buddhist homes, Communist influenced areas, and atheistic backgrounds are being led to walk in the way of salvation."[73]

Today ICC, renamed Ibaraki Christian University,[74] functions as a government school because under missionary oversight it lacked the teaching faculty and financial resources to sustain the rapid growth. Though no longer officially a Christian university, it retains the Christian name and maintains a sincere respect for the missionaries and its Christian legacy that has extended over more than 65 years.

"All for some" is one way to describe Joe's life-long missionary strategy. Quoting the Apostle Paul, Joe often recited, "I have become all things to all men so that by all means I might save some. I do all this for the sake of the gospel."[75]

Becoming "all things to all men" is not becoming a man-pleaser or a manipulator of people. Instead, it is genuinely loving people from one's heart, identifying their areas of felt needs, supplying those basic essentials and, in doing so, earning the right to speak authoritatively into people's lives on the more profound, spiritual level about their greatest need, a reconciled relationship with God through Jesus Christ.

All things . . . to all people . . . so through all means . . . some will be saved. The "all things to all men" strategy extended far beyond the widely effective ministry of Ibaraki Christian College. A remarkable, although

---

72   Joe Cannon personal newsletter, June 22, 1992.

73   Joseph L. Cannon, "ICC Students Seeing the Christian Way", undated article.

74   Specific date of name change in the mid-1960s unknown. An overview of ICC's history and current status as an important Japanese university can be found at: www.icc.ac.jp/english/index.

75   I Corinthians 9:22-23.

incomplete, list of missionary achievements in Japan during the 12 years (1948-1960) of the "Glory Days" include:

KINDERGARTENS

Joe's use of Christian kindergartens as a way to teach youngsters the gospel was an important aspect of his effort. He creatively drafted capable Christian teachers from among local church members and began kindergartens in their church buildings. Costs were covered through modest tuition that parents were pleased to pay in exchange for godly guidance and quality education. Four kindergartens[76] were established in the city of Ibaraki that graduated more than 6,000 children to the next levels of Christian education. Joe modeled for Japanese believers how to use education as a strategic vehicle to advance the gospel, and together they established at least seven[77] independent, locally supported kindergartens that educationally and spiritually cared for more than 400 children at a time.

ORPHANAGES

A distressing, often overlooked tragedy of war is the inevitable collateral consequences inflicted upon children caught in the line of fire. Bombs exploding in neighborhoods wreaked physical devastation upon large sections of many of Japan's largest cities. The obliteration of life and property was emotionally crippling to Japanese society, particularly for children who were directly affected by the loss of family members.

A pressing problem during the early days of Japan's post-war reconstruction was the task of caring for the proliferation of war orphans who were left behind at the end of the war. War orphans were not only those whose parents were killed in the conflict, but also those

---

76 From a missionary brochure entitled "What God Has Done: 20 Years in Japan and Okinawa", 1968.

77 Joe remembered starting kindergartens (pre-schools) in Hitachi, Taga, Omika, Mito, Ichiuchi, Takahangi and Ogitusu. Larry Voyles (Joe's nephew) said these schools were still operating when he visited Japan in 1969.

who were abandoned by families who were unable to care for them. Compounding the trauma of the tragedy was the fact that many of these children were mixed-race, fathered by American servicemen and abandoned when the war ended.

The missionary team worked quickly to establish orphanages devoted to the material and spiritual care of innumerable panic-stricken[78] war orphans.

Once again, the missionaries guided new believers in how to conduct a compassionate, gospel-driven mercy mission among suffering people. Orphanages multiplied as Japanese converts imitated the missionaries and began to initiate their own versions of orphan care. Brother Suzuki, for example, began an orphanage at Nukawa, which cared for and discipled 55 children at a time. Numerous smaller, but similarly successful orphanages began to sprout up along the coastline. Sowa, a brother from Osakadaira, felt compelled to start caring for six orphans in his own home.

RETIREMENT HOMES

One example, among several that could be cited, is that of Brother Kikuchi who established a retirement home in Urizura called "The Garden of Nazareth." This gospel outreach carefully assisted more than 60 people at a time, many of whom were converted to Christ near the end of their lives.

SEWING AND ENGLISH LANGUAGE SCHOOLS

The missionaries constantly brainstormed for new ways to employ educational opportunities as a way to gain people's attention for the gospel. Six sewing schools which emphasized daily Bible lessons, as well as seamstress skills, were scattered throughout the Ibaraki province.

A self-supporting English language night school was started and Joe took a personal interest in sharing Christ with the handfuls of people who wanted to learn English.

78　Even five years following the end of the war, "panic-stricken" was still an apt description of much of Japanese society.

KOREA CAMPAIGNS

Joe loved assisting with gospel work on short-term missions, as he did in Korea. He created opportunities such as this in order to include Japanese believers in cross-cultural mission. This is all the more remarkable considering the historically hostile relationship between Japan and Korea. Joe organized at least three mission trips to Korea in 1953, 1956, and 1967.

Doi-San and Eileen Cannon

RADIO PREACHING

Joe worked closely with Japanese brothers Doi-San and Tokuichi Uza[79] preaching the gospel on a daily program for five years on radio station KSDX. It is said that his fluency in Japanese was so good that local people couldn't tell that he was a foreigner.

YOUTH CAMPS

As one brought to Christ as a young hellion through Camp Omagh in Canada, Joe was passionate, along with other missionaries, about the founding of three youth camps: Motosu Christian Camp (1952), Hitachi Christian Camp (1956), and Sosu Christian Camp (1966).[80]

. . . AND MUCH MORE

Countless ministries flowed out of missionary love for the Japanese people, including compassion for widows, prisoners, and hospital patients. One hospital ministry focused on tuberculosis patients and those who were seriously affected by radiation caused by the

---

79 As of Feb. 1, 2014, Brother Uza, one of Joe's earliest converts, is alive and well, still serving the Lord in Okinawa.

80 *What God Has Done: 20 Years in Japan and Okinawa,* 1968.

war bombings. The happy result is that some of these men, who had been war casualties, were converted to Christ and became gospel preachers themselves.

As Joe believed, it is possible to love the hate out of people and to

Joe with Japanese believers

"overcome evil with good."[81] Genuine love will ultimately win over hardened hearts. The right to speak at deep levels is eventually earned and souls are saved. This is the way the Kingdom advances.

The crowning accomplishment for Joe was that gospel meetings went on simultaneously all over Japan, sometimes as many as 50 annually. The end result of gospel seed sown is always, in God's due time, a harvest of souls saved and churches planted. A conservative estimate is that during these "glory days," more than 3,000 people were converted to Christ. These assembled into at least 35 congregations, spreading even beyond Ibaraki, into the provinces of Tochigi, Fukushima, and as far away as Okinawa.

CANNON SPRIGS

Joe and Rosa Belle's family expanded in some wonderful and unexpected ways while in Japan. Margaret Eileen[82] was the first to arrive on September 5, 1950, at the Tokyo Sanitarium Hospital that was run by the Seventh Day Adventists. Interestingly, a South Pacific typhoon named Eileen made landfall on the east coast of Japan about the time that Eileen was born, thus making the day doubly memorable.[83]

---

81   Romans 12:21.

82   Eileen was named after Joe's sister, Aileen.

83   Nicknamed "Marty" by most of her family and friends, Eileen has worked for many years as a Parts Manager for a Ford Dealership and resides in Virginia.

Over the next six years, however, Joe and Rosa Belle grieved the loss of at least four[84] babies through miscarriages. These were particularly difficult as hospital care in post-war Japan was primitive and RB suffered through the emotional and physical ordeals with limited medical assistance and almost completely without anesthetics.

Joe and RB had hoped for a large family. As previously noted, they were compassionate toward the war-ravaged children in their orphanage ministries. Always alert to do something for the "poorest of the poor" and, believing they were unable to have more children of their own, they applied through Japanese Social Services to adopt a male child. They were sent the names and pictures of two little boys. Unable to choose, Joe and RB joyfully accepted them both.

Joseph Troy,[85] age three, had been born to a Japanese woman and an American serviceman. Joey was from Yokohama where he had lived with his mother, whose father was a Buddhist priest.

Leonard Earl,[86] age one, joined the family a few weeks later. He was from the northern island of Hokkaido and was also fathered by an American military man. Sadly, he had already lived with five foster families before coming to Joe and RB. These two children, Joey and Leonard, were fully accepted into their family with much love by Joe, Rosa Belle and Eileen, in 1956. *[Joey now lives in Bentonville, Arkansas, where he works as a personal trainer and massage therapist. He and his ex-wife have two sons and one daughter. Leonard and his wife Betty live in Douglasville, Georgia, where he has taught civics at a Christian high school.]*

When Joey and Leonard were adopted, Joe and RB were also seeking to adopt a girl through the Holt International Agency in Korea. Joe's interest in Korea stemmed from an experience he had during one of his evangelistic efforts there. One late evening the place where Joe was sleeping was broken into and his only pair of pants was stolen. Joe had

---

84   Rosa Belle experienced at least three other miscarriages prior to Eileen's birth. (Eileen Cannon, e-mail dated January 18, 2014).

85   Joey was named after Joe, Joe's grandfather, Joseph, and RB's older brother Troy.

86   Leonard was named after Joe's father, Leonard, and RB's father Earl.

to borrow a pair of pants from one of the Korean Christians (who was much shorter than Joe). Apparently the pants were many inches too short, making Joe look foolish. A few days later on an extremely cold winter night, Joe crossed paths with a young boy who had no jacket and was apparently a Korean street orphan. Joe struck up a conversation with the child and even gave him his sweater. The next morning Joe was shocked to see the same little boy again, beaten up and the sweater stolen from him. Joe's compassion for Korea's war orphans was greatly stirred by incidents such as this.

A few weeks later, Joe and RB received notice from the Holt Agency that there were no Korean little girls available for adoption, but a picture was included of a baby boy. The child was suffering from malnutrition and covered with open sores. Joe and RB immediately said that they would adopt him. As the paperwork was being finalized for Gregory Paul, they were notified that a little girl, Deborah Ann, had also become available.

This quick succession of additions to the Cannon household was happening just as they prepared for a home visit in the United States

Cannon Family (1958) L to R Deborah, Joe, Leonard, Eileen, Gregory, RB and Joey

so it was determined that Joe and Rosa Belle would take possession of the two latest adoptees there. Gregory Paul, age one, arrived as one of the orphans that the Holt Agency airlifted to Portland, Oregon. RB flew out to personally bring him into the family. *[Greg is married to Rhonda and they have four children. They currently reside in Douglasville, Georgia, where he has been a coach and teacher in a Christian high school.]*

Deborah Ann, age five, was shuttled to Toronto about a month later and was welcomed at the airport with open arms by her new family. Deborah was totally bewildered with exhaustion and culture shock and didn't speak or understand a word of English. Joe spoke only a smattering of Korean but, fortunately for everyone, Deborah became fluent in English quickly. *[Debbie is married to Dave Hogan and they have served for many years as missionaries in Singapore. Dave and Debbie have one daughter, Breda.]*

This is the fascinating story of God's kind providence in bringing two half-Japanese orphans into the Cannon clan in 1956 as well as two half-Korean orphans in 1957 (all fathered by American servicemen).[87] Years later Joe was asked whether or not the four adoptions were consciously made in the wake of their four miscarriages. He replied, "It was not intentional, but it was appropriate."[88]

While on missionary furlough at Abilene Christian College (Abilene, Texas), Rosa Belle unexpectedly became pregnant again. Their return to Japan was delayed while they relocated to Henryetta, Oklahoma, to stay with RB's parents, as they awaited the birth of this next child. Joe stayed busy teaching Bible and Mission at Abilene Christian College, preached at the local Church of Christ, and did some counseling and traveling around to various congregations promoting the work in Japan.

This was a rough time for the Cannon family. It was necessary for Rosa Belle to go on five months bed rest as a precaution to avoid another failed pregnancy. It was a time of high stress, low income, and

---

87   Details of the adoption of Joey and Leonard, from Japan, and Deborah and Gregory, from Korea, provided by Eileen Cannon. Email dated January 18, 2014.

88   Personal interview with Robin Cannon, May 10, 2011.

frequent meals of thinned soup and beans. However, by God's grace, Robin Murray[89] was born healthy and strong on December 19, 1959.

[Robin married Cyndi. They have three children and served as missionaries in Okinawa for 13 years. They presently live in Austin, TX, where Robin works for the World Bible School.]

Following Robin's birth and some recuperation time, the couple and their six children moved back to Japan in 1960. The stirrings of a new challenge for the gospel were rattling around in Joe's head and heart.

MAINLAND JAPAN MISSION SUMMARY

Joe and Rosa Belle were intensely involved in planting indigenous[90] churches on the main island of Japan for three missionary terms from 1948 until 1961.

In their initial four-year term they had concentrated on learning the Japanese language and culture, engaging in gospel preaching, disciple-making, and working with the already established church in the immediate area of Ibaraki and Hitachi City. Joe developed solid friendships with national believers, such as Doi-San, Jugi Watanabe, and Kazuyoshi Mawatari, that became gospel partnerships for many years to come. It was during these first years in Japan that Joe cofounded Ibaraki Christian College.

Their second term had involved a shift of geographic emphasis to the northern part of Japan where the gospel was even less known. They worked closely with brother Mawatari in the strategic city of Sendai, planting a church there and several more north of Sendai along the eastern coastline.

During their third term, while still in the northern region of Japan, brother Doi asked Joe to assist him with preaching the gospel in the

---

89   Robin was named after Joe's life-long, best friend Murray Hammond.

90   The strategy of indigenous church planting is the aim of establishing local congregations that are not missionary-driven, but rather are characterized by being self-governing, self-supporting, and self-propagating.

southernmost extremity. It was on this preaching tour that Joe began to "feel the itch" for going even further south toward Okinawa.

As the decade of the 1950s came to a close, Joe knew that it was time to move along and embrace a new missionary challenge. Japanese believers had begun to lean too heavily upon the missionaries to do what they could—and should by then—be doing for themselves.

After nearly 15 years of hard slogging in a tough ministry in Japan, Joe and Rosa Belle were compelled to shift even further south to the smaller island of Okinawa. However, part of the transition included a one-year furlough serving as a Bible and Mission professor at Abilene Christian College in Texas (1959). Following their stateside assignment they would return to Japan and complete their transition to Okinawa.

The gospel advanced swiftly and the church grew in astonishing ways during those strategic post-war years. The Body of Christ was flourishing in many new places,[91] maturing beautifully, graciously demonstrating the love of Christ, and bringing relief and redemption to war-ravaged Japan.

The "glory days" were glorious because God was glorified.

---

91   In 1949, Dr. and Mrs. Fred Scherman (a dentist), Ed and Edna Brown, and Dr. George and Irene Gurganus joined the missionary team. Following soon were Richard and Mary Baggett, Colis and Delores Campbell, Bill and Norma Carrell, Harold and Gerry Holland, Joe and Bernie Bryant, R.C. and Nona Cannon (no relation to Joe and RB), Max and Mildred Mowrer, Logan and Madelaine Fox, Miss Sarah Andrews, and Miss Hettie Lee Ewing. Bill Harris aspired to join up as well but after three months had to return stateside because his wife refused to join him in "far off" Japan. By the end of the 1950s, more than 42 missionaries were, or had been, working together with the Churches of Christ in Japan. Logan J. Fox, History of Mission Work in Japan, (unpublished), pages 15-18.

PART 3: OKINAWA (1961-1971)

OPERATION ICEBERG

LESS FAMOUS THAN THE BATTLE of the Bulge and Iwo Jima, the World War II Battle of Okinawa was the last and largest[92] of the Pacific island encounters. Codenamed "Operation Iceberg," the American amphibious assault upon Okinawa was a ferocious 82 days[93] of continuous combat.

The furious fight for the control of Okinawa resulted in a massive bloodletting virtually unrivaled in the history of warfare. Japanese troop casualties exceeded 100,000 and more than 50,000 Allied soldiers (primarily American) also perished in the fierce fighting. Tragically, the local people themselves suffered a crushing loss of nearly 150,000 who were either killed, wounded, or attempted suicide during the conflict.[94] Nearly one quarter of the entire civilian populace perished during the invasion, including 39,000 youngsters who were forcibly drafted to assist the Japanese land defensive.[95] "It was a scene straight

---

92   www.factlookup.com/article/Battle_of_Okinawa.

93   April 1-June 21, 1945.

94   Battle of Okinawa, www.GlobalSecurity.org.

95   *The Reader's Companion to Military History,* edited by Robert Cowley and Geoffrey Parker, Houghton Mifflin Harcourt Publishers, 1996. See also www.history.com/topics/battle-of-okinawa.

out of hell. There is no other way to describe it," recalls Tomiko Higa, then a seven-year-old girl who survived the battle.[96]

Okinawa had strategic significance because of its air fields that might be used for future battles. The Allied objective was to seize control of the island from Japan, because of its tactical position in the East China Sea, situated 956 miles south of Tokyo and 855 miles west of Iwo Jima.

Although the Japanese had used kamikaze tactics before, in Okinawa *kamikaze* (intentionally flying their planes into American ships) became their front line of defense. The raw audacity of the suicide pilots caused Vice-Admiral C.R. Brown to dolefully remark, "There was a hypnotic fascination to the sight of kamikazes so alien to our Western philosophy. We watched each plunging kamikaze with the detached horror of one witnessing a terrible spectacle rather than as the intended victim. We forgot self for the moment as we groped hopelessly for the thought of that other man up there."[97]

Sympathetic sentiments were quickly replaced by military responsibility and sheer survival instinct as the Allied forces responded with swift retaliation, resulting in substantial losses on both sides. Fifteen hundred fighter planes and suicide boats slammed their men and machines into the land-approaching Allied forces,[98] causing the U.S. Navy to sustain greater casualties in this single operation than in any other battle of the war.

Allied forces launched their land units and, once ashore, aggression on both sides intensified. Japanese troops hunkered down, embedding themselves inside caves and ancient castles[99] which fortified their de-

---

96   Battle of Okinawa, www.history.com/topics/battle-of-okinawa.

97   John Toland, *The Rising Sun: The Decline & Fall of the Japanese Empire 1936-1945*, Random House, 1970, p. 711.

98   The total strength of the Allied fleet at Okinawa was 1,600 ships, including 40 aircraft carriers, 18 battleships, 32 cruisers and 200 destroyers. In the three-month battle for Okinawa, Japanese kamikaze missions sunk dozens of Allied ships but lost 1,465 of their own planes in the process. Battle of Okinawa, www. GlobalSecurity.org.

99   Castle ruins date from the early 1400s when regional kings fought wars that

fense lines across the north and south length of the island. U.S. foot soldiers ran ashore, advancing as far as they could, crawling and rolling headfirst, with no good place to hide. Unable to even dig holes in the sand because of the lava rock, they crept forward, fully exposed to enemy fire. They managed to take ground steadily, one foot at a time, and often through fierce flurries of bayonet-to-bayonet combat.[100]

Eventually the air fields of Kadena and Yomitan were secured, but not without substantial losses, including both commanding generals. American General Simon B. Buckner was killed by artillery fire, actually a ricocheted bullet. When defeat became certain, Japanese General Ushijima Mitsuru committed suicide.

The final tally of Japanese combatants killed exceeded 107,000, including those who simply blew themselves up with hand grenades and 20,000 more who were sealed in their caves alive (either by their own actions or as a result of battle).[101]

POST-WAR REVERBERATIONS

Punishing grief plagued local Okinawans for years following the island onslaught and even worsened when details of certain war atrocities became public. The Okinawa Prefectural Peace Memorial Museum[102] specifies the crimes:

> [Okinawan deaths] far outnumbered the military death toll. Some were blown apart by shells, some finding themselves

---

eventually led to a unified Kingdom of the Ryukyu Islands. From the article, "Okinawa is Home to Many Castle Ruins" by Chiyomi Sumida (March 12, 2006).

100 The hand-to-hand brawls that ensued along the Cactus Ridge, near the Shuri Line (west central part of the island), have become legendary. The Battle of Okinawa, www.GlobalSecurity.org.

101 History Learning Site: The Battle of Okinawa.

102 The Peace Memorial Museum offers a history of the Battle of Okinawa, including the atrocities that Okinawans endured during the conflict. www.okinawahai.com.

in a hopeless situation were driven to suicide,[103] some died of starvation, and some succumbed to malaria, while others fell victim to the retreating Japanese troops.[104] Under the most desperate and unimaginable circumstances, Okinawans directly experienced the absurdity of war and atrocities it inevitably brings about.

The brittle socio-economics of post-war Okinawa framed the fragile, cultural context into which American missionaries appeared following the war's calamitous conclusion.

FURLOUGH FOLLIES

In the 1950s, Joe and Rosa Belle began to feel strongly compelled to extend their ministry beyond Japan, but they were unsure where to go.[105] Regardless, among the many requisite preparations for their next missionary assignment was an essential pit-stop back in the homeland.

A *furlough* is a military term for "rest and relaxation" (R & R) that implies a temporary withdrawal from the intensity of frontline battle. Missionaries appropriately use *furlough* to describe a vital purpose of their occasional home visits. But, for most missionaries, furloughs become the busiest and most stressful times of their lives. A well-tested

---

103 "Driven to suicide" is described as the Japanese Army "directing civilians to commit suicide and being handed grenades by soldiers, to blow themselves apart." Civilian citizens, induced by Japanese propaganda to believe that U.S. soldiers were barbarians who committed horrible atrocities, killed their own families and themselves to avoid American capture. Some of them threw themselves and their family members from the cliffs where the Peace Museum now resides. www.peace-museum.pref.okinawa.jp.

104 "Soldiers on both sides raped Okinawan civilians, and rape by the Japanese troops became common after it became clear the Japanese had been defeated." *Japan's Battle of Okinawa*, April-June, 1945, Thomas M. Huber.

105 They considered a new ministry in such places as South Korea, Taiwan, Vietnam, China, and the Philippines. Joe even made a trip to Brazil to explore the possibility of working in the city of San Paulo, the fourth largest Japanese- speaking city in the world.

witticism about missionary home visits cleverly says, "We have to get back to the field to get a rest."

Rather than R & R, "running with the bulls"[106] is a more apt description of a missionary time-out. Joe viewed furloughs as an occupational nuisance. But he reasoned if the ministry must be disrupted, at least let it be leveraged to raise up the necessary "prayer-power, money-power, and man-power" to further the work. Because whatever Joe did he did full steam forward, stateside travels were attacked with purpose and enthusiasm.

The first Cannon "Bull Run" (furlough) included three-year-old Eileen in 1953. The traveling threesome logged many tough miles in various regions of the U.S. and Canada, visiting family and supporting churches.

Joe didn't go to churches merely to preach sermons. The Cannons arrived with two ragged brown suitcases full of artifacts showcasing Japanese history and culture. It was show-and-tell time with a map of Japan pinned to the wall! Joe wowed the small congregations with exciting stories and pictures depicting life and gospel advances in Japan. Usually Eileen sang Japanese songs, dressed in a red and white kimono, complete with silk-sock booties (split for the big toe) and wooden, platform sandals.

Usually Joe overbooked his itinerary. Once he was scheduled to preach at the Omagh church outside Toronto. Because his plane was delayed, he didn't have time to retrieve his luggage. He arrived at the church well into an extended song service, still wearing his wrinkled travel clothes. Joe barged through the door, surveyed the crowd, and located a man about his size. He quickly borrowed the man's jacket and stepped into the pulpit without missing a beat.[107]

The Cannons often gave small gifts from Japan to those who hosted them on their church-hopping journeys. On one visit to the family farm in Henryetta, Oklahoma, Joe gave his father-in-law Earl an 18-inch tobacco pipe. It had a steel bowl and a tip with a bamboo stem.

---

106 The Running of the Bulls is a dangerous part of the Festival of San Fermin in Pamploma, Spain, held in July of every year, dating back to the 13th century.

107 Larry Voyles "Cannon Notes" (September 15, 2011).

Earl smoked Prince Albert tobacco in it for years before learning it was made to be an opium pipe![108]

Their 1953 furlough ended with a flurry of humorous travel anecdotes and many tearful goodbyes before they hurried back for another five-year stint in the "Land of the Rising Sun."

Their second "Bull Run" furlough centered around Abilene, Texas, where Joe studied toward a Master's degree at Abilene Christian College.[109] A Cannon custom was to bring one or two Japanese church leaders home with them on furloughs. Joe joyfully escorted them around to various congregations and provided them with occasions to preach. Red-faced and with arms flailing, Joe enthusiastically translated their messages into English. The churches were invigorated and freshly challenged by getting to know their Japanese brothers and by seeing living fruit of the gospel's progress in the Orient. Mitsugu Doi[110] and Mawatari San, from the city of Sendai, were two leaders who accompanied the Cannon clan stateside in 1959.

By this time, the family had grown to five with Eileen and the newly adopted Japanese/American boys, Joey and Leonard. However, prior to leaving Japan, Deborah and Gregory, both Korean/American, were unexpectedly approved by the adoption agency. The suddenness of this good news made it practical to receive Debbie and Greg into the family while on home leave in the United States.

Less than a year later, another surprise arrived with the birth of Robin, increasing the family to six children under the age of nine, by the end of 1959. Rosa Belle's difficult pregnancy with Robin had delayed their departure for Japan. However, once back, they quickly readied themselves for a ministry transition further south.

---

108 Larry Voyles "Family Reminisces" (undated).

109 Joe completed his M.A. at Harding College in Searcy, AR, in 1969.

110 Mitsugu Doi had trained to be a kamikaze war pilot. However, the war ended before he was deployed. He was among the first converts of Joe's missionary team in 1947.

ISLAND HOP

The gospel had gotten off to a great start for the Churches of Christ in Okinawa in 1952 through the stalwart efforts of Brother Saito, one of Joe's early converts in Japan and a recent graduate of Ibaraki Christian College. As interest in the evangelization of Okinawa increased, Joe and Rosa Belle were overjoyed by the readiness of Japanese congregations to assist in spearheading gospel growth into the southern Ryukyu Islands.

In 1960, Joe preached a series of gospel meetings in Okinawa and was elated by the faith and eagerness of the believers there who began to put the "friendly squeeze" on him and RB to move south. Joe sent a typically straightforward letter[111] to their home churches to explain the decision to shift their emphasis to Okinawa: "The first and most important consideration is the command of Christ and the providence of God. We have been led to this decision in ways that are impossible to deny."

Joe's list of "providences" included the fact that Japanese congregations were becoming overly dependent upon the missionaries, the strong and specific appeal of Okinawan believers for assistance, the educational needs of [the missionaries'] children[112] and, most importantly, the inward compelling of the Holy Spirit that it was time to open a new field of work for the gospel. Joe concluded, "We could not resist the strong pull [of Christ] toward Okinawa. God has blessed us in Japan, and has given us fruit and happiness in our work here. If it is his will, we hope to remain in this field of endeavor for the rest of our lives."

Once convinced of direction, Joe and RB confidently made a run for it.

---

111 August 4, 1962.

112 The U.S. military base on Okinawa provided good educational opportunities and preempted the possible necessity of returning stateside for an extended period of time.

VALIANT VISION

A strategic visionary, Joe was always scheming to take the gospel to "the regions beyond."[113] Choosing to relocate in Okinawa in no way diminished his desire for the many other places where he aspired to advance the name of Christ. He was hardly unpacked before looking beyond his new island home to faraway gospel targets.

A missionary brochure described Okinawa:

> . . . from its geographical position along the shores of Red China, Okinawa can be the springboard for spreading the gospel to many other places. By air, Okinawa is only two hours from Formosa (Taiwan), three hours from the Philippines and Seoul, Korea, six hours from Vietnam, and only thirty minutes away is the Chinese mainland.

> In addition to all this, the souls of 1,000,000 Ryukyuan[114] people, including 80,000 Americans (military) can be touched for Christ on the island of Okinawa.[115]

OKINAWA PARTNERSHIPS

By September 1962 five young Okinawan preachers[116] were struggling to care for five infant congregations spread around the southern por-

---

113 2 Corinthians 10:16

114 The Ryukyus are a group of 55 islands of southwest Japan extending from the southernmost island of Kyushu to the northern tip of Taiwan. Okinawa is the largest and most important island of the Ryukyus. Information collected from the American Heritage Dictionary, the Britannica Concise Encyclopedia, and the Columbia Encyclopedia.

115 Quoted from a Church of Christ missionary brochure entitled, "Okinawa: The Keystone of the Pacific" (1964).

116 "It is noteworthy to mention the faithful labors of our Christian brothers, Tokuichi Uza, Tomoyose, Junichi Akamine, Seisho Arakaki, and Yoshihiro Nakamura." Joe Cannon missionary report, September 4, 1962.

tion of the island. The need was for experienced leadership to reinforce the efforts of these hardworking national brothers who would then facilitate expansion of the gospel into more remote areas.

The Ojana military congregation had its own building with a revolving membership of about 150 members who rotated in and out as their assignments changed. The five Okinawan congregations were smaller and struggling. The Naha congregation num-

Tokuichi and Tsuruko Uza

bered about 25 who met in their own small building. The others were home congregations at Ishikawa, Itoman, Maehara, and Ojana ranging in size from five to fifteen believers.[117] Each of these towns had been locations of vicious fighting near the end of World War II. The arrival of the Cannon family infused a burst of enthusiasm and energy into these fledgling efforts. In typical whirlwind fashion, Joe swooped in on a Saturday and preached Sunday, once in Japanese to the Naha congregation and later in English to the military congregation at Ojana.

An insight into Joe's philosophy of teamwork in church planting shines through in a September 1962 report:

> The influx of new workers [Joe and RB] now makes it possible to spread the gospel to new areas. A team effort is being made to start a new congregation in the Tomari area of Naha, with brother Uza spearheading the drive. The same kind of effort is to be made in the city of Koza, with brother Arakaki leading.

---

117 Statistical information provided in the *Christian Chronicle, Vol. XX, No. 7, Nov. 16, 1962.*

Along with the effort to establish two new churches, several gospel meetings are being planned, new Bible classes have started . . . Bible Correspondence Courses (in Japanese) are being prepared, radio programs are afoot, visitation work[118] is being stepped up, and a gospel paper is being published.

This is classic Joe Cannon. One of Joe's endearing qualities was his quickness to publicly recognize the efforts of others when the gospel succeeded in new places. He didn't just do the work; he energized and prepared others to do it. In the process, he accelerated the progress of the gospel.

Joe's work with the emerging national leadership stretched far beyond Bible training and other strictly spiritual exercises. He was insistent that national men, sooner rather than later, develop into frontrunners who could lead their congregations forward in the work of Christ. He devoted thousands of hours, over decades of evenings, mentoring men in practical essentials[119] of local church leadership.

After one year in Okinawa, through hard work and despite heartache, three new congregations were established with at least 40 conversions to Christ. The "glory days" of gospel receptiveness seemed to follow Joe as he organized 12 more gospel meetings throughout the following year.[120]

STRUCK DOWN, BUT NOT DESTROYED[121]

In the early 1960s, the Cannons' thriving ministry collided with a succession of crushing personal losses, the first of which affected the

---

118 Visitation work means orphanages, retirement centers, hospitals, schools, and lepersoriums. In Japan the missionaries started these mercy ministries, however in Okinawa the government had already started them. Joe mobilized the Okinawan believers to use them as means to demonstrate the love of Christ.

119 How to conduct business meetings, prepare budgets, provide financial accountability, reports, etc.

120 Joe Cannon missionary report, January 8, 1964.

121 2 Corinthians 4:9.

family in a distressing, long-term way. Ivy Rose Cannon[122] was the last of the Cannon children. Born in Naha, Okinawa, on November 11, 1961, she died suddenly six weeks later on December 17.

The official cause of death was "crib death." (The present-day term of Sudden Infant Death Syndrome or SIDS was unknown at that time.) No autopsy was performed and Ivy Rose was buried the following day.[123]

Less than five months later on May 9, 1962, Joe's father died from a rare disease, Wegener's Granulomatosis.[124] Leonard was 62. In a letter to Joe his mother Ivy quoted the coroner[125] who said there were only 58 recorded cases of Granulomatosis in medical history, with no known origin or cure for the disease.

After Leonard's death, Ivy moved to Okinawa and became a refreshing addition to the Cannon household. Unfortunately, Ivy died of breast cancer only three years later on February 7, 1965.

Several insights into the everyday reality of Joe's faith during the Okinawa days were related to me by Don Brown:[126]

> You couldn't be around Joe for very long without getting your faith challenged, in a good way . . . you'd go away strengthened just by listening to him.

---

122 Ivy Rose was named after Joe's mother Ivy.

123 After Joe's mother Ivy died in 1965, she was interred at the same location in Naha, Okinawa. A few years later, both graves were relocated to the Naha International Cemetery in order to make room for a road extension.

124 Frederick Wegener first described this disease in 1936. Because of his Nazi past, professional bodies and journals often drop or replace "Wegener" from the disease name.

125 A letter dated July 13, 1962 is included with the official autopsy report conducted by Dr. Mautner.

126 Don was an American civilian, employed by the military in Okinawa in 1965, working on the development of the HALT (Highly Accelerated Life Testing) Missile System. Edited from an audio interview.

My first Sunday in Okinawa I attended the Ojana military congregation. When it was time for the sermon, this fellow sauntered over to the pulpit. There was no mention of his name . . . He just started preaching. His wavy hair was turning grey, very distinguished, and I thought he was a sergeant or something . . . And he was all over that pulpit, he might have put his hands on it once in a while, but he would walk off to one side and then the other . . . He was telling about his mother who had died just the week before. But his attitude was like something I had never seen before. He was so happy because his mother had died and was now in heaven! And I thought, well, that's the way we're supposed to feel. But Joe really does feel that way . . . The man simply doesn't fear [a believer's] death . . . Joe often said, "If I die on the mission field, bury me where I fall. The Lord knows where to find me!"

The military warned us about dangerous snakes on the island. One night, I was sitting on Joe's patio . . . And we were talking about the large and extremely venomous Habu[127] snakes. I don't like snakes and expressed my concern about them. Joe was cooking weenies on the grill and he looks over at me, and says, "Snakes!? Why are you worried about snakes? The Lord will take care of you. Son, you can't go through life worrying about snakes!"

Joe literally lived by faith. One time, Joe and RB showed up unexpectedly at the Texarkana, Texas, congregation in 1965 . . . Relating the story, Joe said to me, "Don, RB and I had seven cents between us, and we put it in the collection plate. After the service, the elders met with me and they gave us $300. I didn't even preach that day and I certainly didn't ask for the money. But the Lord provided." Here's the thing . . . Joe didn't worry about

127 A relative species to the cobra.

the things I worry about. He just believes the Lord will always provide for him; the Lord does provide for him, and so, it's just never been an issue. That doesn't mean Joe and RB didn't have hardships . . . Lots of them . . . They're just undaunted by them.

Larry Voyles, in notes collected for this book, recalls a "discernible shift from Joe's usual free-spirit persona–into a deep, spiritual humility when he prayed or talked to someone about the gospel." Joe could morph from boisterous laughter and horseplay almost instantly into a reverent personal conversation with the Lord. He was a practical jokester but was always poised for spontaneous, intensely serious and spiritual discussions.

However, Joe and Rosa Belle were not spiritual superheroes. For quite some time after the death of Ivy Rose, the jovial Joe gave way to solemnity. Rosa Belle went into a debilitating depression, spent long periods in bed, and began to experience severe pain in her neck and back.

When Joe's mother moved to Okinawa, her presence became a great relief to Rosa Belle. Ivy was able to manage the household tasks and care for the children. This allowed Joe to travel with RB to the U.S. for an unscheduled, but timely, visit to the Mayo Clinic in Minnesota.

The time away was helpful, but the end results were disappointing. Because RB's pain issues were depression-related, they were not easy to treat. She was essentially counseled to "just get over it." They returned to Okinawa and Rosa Belle slowly emerged from her oppressive gloom after about four years. Meanwhile Joe overworked himself into an emotional and physical frazzle, possibly suffering an undiagnosed nervous breakdown as well.

Although the Cannon family endured considerable grief while in Okinawa, particularly during the first half of the 1960s, God's grace was sufficient. They persevered and continued carrying the gospel forward throughout the remainder of the decade.

CHURCH PLANTING HIGHLIGHTS

Okinawa was an exotic island sandbox for the Cannon kids to grow up in during the mid-1960s. Leonard and Joey remember exploring famous war sites. Once they found an entrance into some of the caves where Japanese soldiers barricaded themselves to ward off the advancing Allied troops. Nearly 20 years after the end of World War II, the boys were still finding human remains, helmets, hand grenades, and other war trophies. One day, they found an unexploded bomb in their swimming hole! Joe informed the bomb squad who retrieved a 16-inch, two-ton naval shell.[128]

On the Japanese mainland Joe and Rosa Belle had worked closely with a team of North American missionaries and, later, with Japanese nationals. But in Okinawa, there weren't any other expatriate missionaries. Joe and RB aligned themselves closely with the existing local leadership of the five congregations there. This was a happy reunion— to now work as colleagues with men who were once disciples from their earlier ministry in Japan. Okinawa was a pleasant continuation of work that Joe and Rosa Belle always considered a joyful privilege.

Evangelism through educational institutions remained a successful strategy, as it had been on the mainland of Japan. More than 4,000 students walked the campus of Okinawa University every day. The school was wide open and Joe walked into it. He earned a full professorship at Okinawa University that carried with it credentials necessary to engage students on campus with various forms of religious instruction. Joe taught a six-hour course on the "The English Bible as Literature" as part of the university curriculum. He also directed the Christian Students Association which allowed him access to high school students as well as collegians. Joe's eagerness to work with students was the start of the Okinawan Christian Education Center, which led to his outreach on another college campus and resulted in many students coming to Christ.

---

128 Larry Voyles "Family Reminisces" (undated).

An evangelistic church planting missionary, Joe didn't adhere to regular office hours and hated busy work. His passion was to be a man of the Word and prayer and to be available to those with the least access to the gospel.

Stories such as the following encouraged Joe to continue his weekly evangelistic messages for KSDX (1250) Radio which was also carried on the Far-East Radio Broadcasting Company. A Filipino fisherman first heard the gospel as a result of these programs. In His meticulous providence, God led the man directly to Okinawa and to a small Bible study Joe was teaching:

> Three years languishing in a Red China jail had brought the fishing boat crew great despair. Fellow prisoners were dying all around them. "Why had the shaft on their boat broken, causing them to drift into Communist waters, only to be picked up and accused of spying?"

> One day, while still in prison, Tamamoto somehow received a small book containing the stories of Esther and Ruth from a Chinese doctor. This was his first contact with the Word of God.

> After his release from prison he listened to a religious broadcast from Manila on the ship radio. Then, when he [happened] to be in port at Itoman (Okinawa), he sought out the radio preacher by attending a Bible class advertised on the program.

> Noboru Tamamoto heard and believed the gospel and is thankful to God whose Word became a light in the darkness, leading him from the imprisonment of men and Satan into the glorious liberty of the children of God.[129]

---

129 Adapted from Joe Cannon article in *Power for Today (undated)*.

As the decade of the 1960s came to an end, Joe was busy writing, planting churches, and making frequent journeys back and forth to mainland Japan encouraging the churches he planted there.

Joe's writing ministry included Japanese commentaries on Philemon, Jude, and Galatians and his first book, *For Missionaries Only*, written partly in Okinawa and finished while on furlough in 1969 in Searcy, Arkansas.

The 1968-69 furlough was the only one shared by the entire family during the decade of the 1960s. But it was a happy one! Joe and RB purchased a new 1968 Volkswagen van and drove it from one end of North America to the other (Ottawa, Canada to Vancouver, Washington) visiting such memorable vacation spots as Yellowstone National Park. Other than that, Joe made two emergency trips stateside during the 1960s, once for his father's funeral and once for Rosa Belle to be seen at the Mayo Clinic.

MISSION PREPARE!

Joe received an exciting invitation from his alma mater, Harding College, to serve as the Visiting Professor of Missions for the 1969 school year. A key feature of *Mission Prepare* was the employment of a full-time missionary on the faculty to vigorously promote cross-cultural mission. When asked about this mission opportunity, Joe was unable to contain his true feelings:[130] "Words cannot express my delight in seeing realized a training program for our missionary evangelists. My soul has been vexed at the almost total neglect of missionary training in past years. *Mission Prepare* heralds a great day for the fulfilling of the commission of our Lord to make disciples of all the nations."

I can't be certain, but I believe Joe already had in mind another ministry transition on the near horizon. Therefore, it was imperative that they get back to the home churches to firm up their prayer and financial resources in preparation for another unflinching gospel advance "to

---

the end of the earth."[131] In a letter to his supporters, he commends them for their long investment in their work in Japan and Okinawa:[132]

Mission Prepare! Harding College (1969)

> I guess you realize that we have worked together for more than twenty years now. Many of those who started with us have preceded us to heaven. Others have dropped their support for various reasons . . . We want to honor those of you who have never quit. You have what it takes to do the work of Christ. You see more than immediate success. You are willing to let patience have its perfect work . . .There are hundreds of Christians and many churches existing now because we stuck it out together. Not that I think it is perfectly done and over. Nor do I think we are something apart from the grace of Christ.

> It is our intention to return to the work here . . . My wife and I gave our lives to the work of the gospel a long time ago, and we intend to stick with the work as long as Christ will put up with us. We hope you can put up with us also . . .

The Cannon family returned to Okinawa in late 1969, following a good year at Harding College. Eileen remained in Searcy to attend Harding College. Joe and Rosa Belle had solidified their support base and were eager to get back to the missionary front line.

---

131   Acts 1:8.

132   November 30, 1968 (adapted quote).

NO MORE PLACE FOR ME IN THESE REGIONS[133]

As I conclude this chapter on Joe and Rosa Belle's nearly 25 years of ministry in the Orient, it is significant to make note and appreciate another winsome quality about Joe. He was never one to tell only the good stuff. He insisted on reporting both the good news and bad. As Joe broadly summarized nearly 25 years in Japan and Okinawa, he honestly acknowledged the advances and setbacks, the ebbs and flows of mission:

> Did all of our converts remain faithful? No. Did all of the churches we planted survive and continue on? No. But with many setbacks, problems and hardships, the gospel has gone forward.[134]

> In and Out. This was and is the story of Japanese Christians. Baptize ten, lose ten. Baptize ten, lose nine. Baptize ten, lose five. Baptize none, lose none. How hard it is for them to buck their pagan society. How great their tribulations have been! We can criticize, but can we understand? We can be disillusioned with them, but can we bear with them? Some of these children last about as long in the faith as their fathers do in the field. They are as true to Christ as their teachers are to them. But alas, this is only partly true, for some leave sooner. But thanks be to God, some never leave.[135]

Joe and Rosa Belle were eager to roll along to their next assignment from the Lord of the harvest. This time Joe became strangely stirred by what he was learning about the island of New Guinea.

---

133 Romans 15:23.

134 Joseph L. Cannon, undated newsletter (late 1960s).

135 Joseph L. Cannon, *For Missionaries Only, Baker Book House (1969), pages 8-9.*

STRANGELY STIRRED

An exit strategy was always part of Joe and Rosa Belle's vision of ministry. They never proposed to start churches and pastor them for the rest of their lives. Joe was Apostle Paul-like in many ways, and this is one of them. He didn't want to begin as a gospel *pioneer*, but end up as a *settler*.

The nine years on Okinawa were among the best and worst of their lives. Intertwined with exciting gospel advance, churches established, and the joy of local leaders taking charge of their care, the Cannons also grieved several family deaths, especially the tragic circumstances surrounding Ivy Rose. Joe and RB had endured some arduous years in Okinawa and forged through debilitating discouragements. However, once they returned to Okinawa, following furlough, the anticipated itch for a new gospel challenge came hard and fast.

Once Joe determined that Okinawan congregations were strong enough to carry on without him, he had become strangely stirred for the island of New Guinea. When he happened upon a *National Geographic* article about newly discovered highlands tribes, he was compelled by what he believed were the Lord's "orders from headquarters" for his next missionary task. Not only did Joe want to go to New Guinea, he sought Japanese and Okinawan churches to help him spearhead the effort:

> We believe God has called us to lead the Church of Christ into this kind of missionary work. Up to now, the 70 churches in Japan (including Okinawa) have not done any foreign mission work. We want to challenge them with what needs to be done for Christ in New Guinea. We also want to challenge the American and Canadian church to enter into this most difficult field, to sacrifice and achieve advancement for the Lord Jesus Christ.[136]

---

136 *The Oracle*, a weekly bulletin of the West Toronto Church of Christ, December 6, 1970.

Not everyone was enthralled by the prospect of a venture into New Guinea. Before Joe went public with the announcement, at least one prominent Church of Christ leader, Dr. George Gurganus, wrote Joe a letter in which he bluntly stated, "The thought of your leaving Okinawa leaves me cold. I wish you could see your way open to remaining there . . . Of course, we also need a good work in northern Japan."[137]

Tokuichi Uza was one of Joe's early converts in Japan, and they later worked together in Okinawa. Brother Uza visited Dr. Gurganus in Abilene, Texas, about this time, and they evidently had an entertaining conversation regarding Joe's decision to leave the Orient for a new endeavor in Papua New Guinea. Brother Uza, with his endearing use of English, said, "He [Dr. Gurganus] hate you for leave from Japanese speaking people. I do too."[138]

This, of course, was good-natured jesting. George and Brother Uza had such personal concern for the evangelization of Japan and Okinawa that they hated to see good missionaries leave. But within months, George and Uza became convinced of the importance of reaching Papua New Guinea for Christ and encouraged Joe and RB to go, something Joe was eager to do.

In the years following, an impressive number of Japanese congregations financially supported and prayed for the gospel to spread quickly in Papua New Guinea (PNG) and several[139] joined the Cannons there. It was a level of support that Joe and RB were rightfully pleased about, especially because it came from so many who were themselves new to the family of God.

---

137   Letter dated October 19, 1970. George and Irene Gurganus were missionary colleagues with Joe and RB in Japan for two terms of work.

138   Letter dated December 7, 1970.

139   Hideki Ataka, Kyoko Fukuda, Etsuko Saito, Nagisa Oksaka, and Teruko Suzuki were among those who worked with Joe in PNG. They served the Lord well during their years in PNG. Hideki later married Nagisa, and they continue to work with the Hitachi Church of Christ in Hitachi, Japan.

PART 4: PAPUA NEW GUINEA (1971-1984)

FIJIAN MISSIONARIES HEROICALLY *EKBALLOED* [140] themselves onto New Guinea's southern shore in 1874.

Missionary John Williams became one of the first non-nationals to establish the gospel in the French Polynesian Islands in the early 1830s, most notably on the island of Raiatea. However, when the London Missionary Society refused his request to move toward the more unreached islands further west, he became an unhappy missionary.[141] Williams fumed, "Why should you confine me within a single reef when there are hundreds of islands whose people have not heard the gospel? If the board won't shift me, then I'm going to shift myself!"

He built his own ship and took a group of national missionaries from Raiatea on board with enough food and supplies for a 3,000 mile voyage. His plan was to plot a course west across the South Pacific, assigning two Raiatea evangelists to every island that the Lord brought into their path.

---

140   *Ekballo* is the Greek word for "send out" in Matthew 9:38 and Luke 10:2. Ekballo means to "forcibly expel; hurl; fling; propel." It is the same word used for "casting out" demons in Matthew 10:1. This concept of being "forcefully flung" by the Lord of the harvest, into mission, through prayer, was not unfamiliar to Joe. *Ekballo* is yellow and red highlighted in both the Matthew and Luke texts in his Interlinear Greek-English New Testament.

141   The following story is adapted from Alan R. Tippett, *The Deep-Sea Canoe*, William Carey Library, Pasadena, CA (1977), pages 38-41.

John Williams personally approached the chieftain in each place and preached Christ to them. He asked the chiefs, "If I leave one of my teachers to tell you more of the gospel, will you receive him?" If the leader said yes, he left Raiatean missionaries on the island. Then he sailed on toward Tonga, Samoa, Fiji, and New Guinea.

During one of these relentless gospel excursions, Williams was killed and eaten by cannibals on the island of Erromango[142] in November 1839.[143] However, the national missionaries refused to halt their mission just because their leader had been cannibalized! They eagerly pressed on, preaching the gospel, moving continually westward.

It took nearly 25 years for the coastal areas of Fiji to be won to Christ. Then they turned their attention to the interior regions until footholds for the gospel were also gained there. Another 25 years of persistent church planting were required before the message of Christ was known throughout the islands of Fiji. A vital observation is that virtually all of this gospel pioneering was accomplished by courageous, life-risking Fijian believers in the midst of incredibly fierce peoples in the interior mountains.

By the late 1860s the Fijian church began asking itself, "When all of our people have turned from their old religion, is our mission finished?" They answered their own question with a resounding "No! We must go to the uttermost islands where Christ is still unknown!"

But how did the gospel get to New Guinea?

Fiji became a British Colony in 1874. The church in Fiji initiated an alliance with the church in Australia, forming a partnership to push Christianity farther west toward the island of New Guinea. Australian believers served as senders, providing the financial support for Fijian believers who were eager to be the gospel goers.

Just about the time the first missionaries were ready to launch, Fiji was abruptly crippled by a measles plague that spread through the

---

142   An island in the New Hebrides island chain.

143   Rev. James J. Ellis. *John Williams: The Martyr Missionary of Polynesia (1900)*. S.W. Partridge & Co. LTD, London.

islands, killing more than 40,000 people. In one place, more than 200 pastors and teachers perished during the epidemic. The devastating disease caused many to question how they could proceed with the mission when they hardly had a sufficient number of Christian leaders remaining to carry on the local work.

An Australian brother, Dr. Brown, head of the Australian Mission Board arrived in Fiji on the first ship allowed into port following the catastrophe. He became heartsick at such widespread loss of life. Discouraged, but not dissuaded from the urgency of the gospel cause, he remarked, "I hardly have the heart to ask these people to give up some of their very few teachers and pastors who are still alive, but I will go to the theological institution, in case there are some who will still go."

Dr. Brown addressed the students saying, "You know how we planned to have a mission to New Guinea. But you have suffered so much from the measles outbreak and have lost so many people that I really don't know what to do. But I wonder if there is perhaps *someone* among you who would still volunteer to go to New Guinea."

The principal of the school replied, "Let's not ask them to make a decision this moment. Let them think it over and tomorrow we will talk again."

The students conferred with their wives and prayed through the evening. In the morning 84 theological students gathered together and sat silently. The principal stood and simply asked, "I would like to know if anyone among you is still willing to go to New Guinea? If so, please stand." Every one of the 84 stood up!

A government administrator became concerned that possibly the students were being improperly coerced. He encouraged them not to go, saying, "You need not go unless you want to." But the students remained firm in their decisions. The administrator persisted even more stridently, trying to deter them. "Do you people want to die in a foreign land?" Dr. Brown wrote a journal entry stating that when the question was so forcefully proposed, he feared that surely the students would reconsider their choice.

However, one of the Fijian students, Aminio Baledrokadroka, stood to speak. He persuasively restated the unanimous resolution of the students, "We have fully considered the matter and our minds are made up. No one has pressed us in any way. We have heard the call of God, we have given ourselves to God's work, and it is our mind to go to New Guinea. If we live, we live. If we die, we die."[144]

This young band of Fijian families built their own coffins, packed personal belongings into them and sailed thousands of miles, on phenomenal voyages across the South Pacific in their deep-sea canoes,[145] arriving in New Guinea in 1874.

Successive groups of Fijian missionaries were wiped out by malarial fevers and hostile New Guinea tribes. But when one team was obliterated, another set of martyr missionaries stepped into the gap to replace them. Eventually, through many hardships and persecutions, the gospel was finally planted in the coastal areas of New Guinea. But a lot of life was laid down for the Name!

One party of Fijian missionaries was led by Sailasa Naucukidi.[146] Sailasa guided the evangelists into the mountains of New Ireland where they were almost immediately killed, cooked in the cannibal furnaces and eaten. When word of the slaughter reached Fiji, Sailasa's own brother inquired, "Who were the missionaries killed?" He was told, "Your brother was one of them." Instead of becoming angry, he bowed his head and said, "I am going to take his place as a missionary in New Guinea." He built a coffin and headed to New Guinea himself.

---

144 I am indebted to Alan R. Tippett (1911-1988) for much of this history of the Fijian mission to New Guinea. Dr. Tippett was an Australian missiologist, anthropologist, and 20-year veteran missionary to Fiji. Missiological research took him to Mexico, the Solomon Islands, Polynesia, Ethiopia, and Navajo Indian reservations in North America.

145 Deep-sea canoes were huge, double canoes sporting wide, wing-like sails. Some canoes were even longer than Captain Cook's ship, the Endeavor. Alan R. Tippett, The Deep-Sea Canoe, William Carey Library, Pasadena, CA (1977), page 9.

146 Alan R. Tippett, The Deep-Sea Canoe, William Carey Library, Pasadena, CA (1977), page 68-69.

Such was the courage and conviction of the Fijian missionaries. When asked if they were afraid to die for Christ, the standard response became, "We died before we left!" These fearless Fijians were the first wave of the first responder missionaries in New Guinea. But they were not to be the last. There are hundreds of stories like this with equally grisly details. It is fitting for a biography of Joe Cannon to salute those faithful Fijians who laid the foundation in New Guinea from which he benefitted.

NEW GUINEA CALL AND RECONNAISSANCE

Around the northern tip of Okinawa is a scenic retreat and summer camp site known as Camp Sosu. The camping area is beautifully situated in a secluded mountainous area perched along a high point overlooking rocky cliffs, crashing waves, and wide-open ocean. In February of 1970,[147] Joe Cannon and Flint Garrison and their families withdrew there for a few days of vacation.

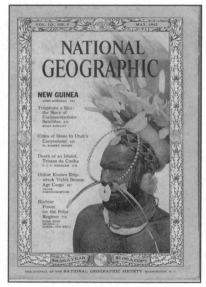

National Geographic (May 1962)

The two families enjoyed pleasant evenings talking or singing around a roaring campfire. Late one night, Joe brought out an article that he had clipped from a *National Geographic* magazine. The feature article described the early 1960s discovery of more than one million stone-aged people previously unknown to the world. Joe and Flint were intrigued

---

147   Joseph L. Cannon, *The Experiences of a New Guinea Pig* (1974), page 9, Hall Publishing House, Texarkana, TX. In this book, the date of the family retreat is February 1971. I have concluded from Joe's newsletters and other correspondence that the year was actually 1970.

by the article with its exotic, colorful pictures. They agreed that the one thing needed most by the primitive people in New Guinea was a knowledge of Christ and the gospel. They ended up praying through most of the night. Sometime in the early morning hours, Joe committed himself to seek the Lord further about what he should personally do about New Guinea.

In the following months, Joe and Rosa Belle were unable to shirk the obvious compelling of the Holy Spirit. On October 20, 1970, they determined to target New Guinea. Three days later Joe made their intentions public in a brief newsletter[148] to their supporters:

> After much thought and prayer, we have decided to move to New Guinea and work among the mountain tribes there. For some time now, we have desired to pioneer a work in a region where no one has ever preached Christ. New Guinea is one of those last places in the world with areas unexplored, and peoples yet unreached with the gospel.

Joe frequently composed poetry and songs to express his deepest longings. Later that same day, Joe wrote from his heart:

There is someone out there waiting, who has never heard of Christ

There is someone out there dying, who must face eternal loss

Can I sit in easy comfort and ignore the plaintive cry?

Can I live for self and safety, when the world's about to die?

Can I turn from bloody Calvary and seek the easy way

When he died for me and saved me, changing all my night to day?

No! I've got to face the issue of the work yet to be done

Yes! I've got to take my cross until the victory is won

---

148   October 23, 1970.

So, hold on Oh child in bondage for the Word is drawing nigh!
You shall hear the gospel story and no longer shall you die!

Joe Cannon, October 23, 1970

A few days before Christmas 1970, Joe received a deflating letter informing him:

> We [the church] have no idea where we can get the $1,000 you need for the New Guinea survey trip. All of the elders have read your letter regarding the matter, but no plan has been devised to raise it.[149]

Evidently Joe got the money somewhere. He booked a flight[150] and headed solo for the island of New Guinea armed only with a map and the name of a young Australian, Rick Niland. In Joe's mind this was not merely a survey trip to determine whether or not they were moving to New Guinea. Rather, he was on mission to pinpoint a definite location to live and base the ministry.

Upon arrival in Port Moresby, Joe received the often repeated pioneer greeting: "No friends, no brothers and no welcome," as noted in a journal entry.[151] Not quite the same reception the Fijians received 104 years earlier, but still noteworthy. However, Joe wasn't friendless for long. Rick Niland radioed Joe the news that he was soon to arrive in Port Moresby to meet him.

Joe and Rick enjoyed five days together in the capital city of Port Moresby in what was then the Territory of New Guinea.[152] Rick was a 26-year-old Australian, who had joined the government service as

---

149 Letter from Cliff Cobb, on behalf of the Orient St. Church of Christ Elders (Stamford, TX), dated Dec. 15, 1970.

150 January 10, 1971.

151 Mid-January, 1971. Joe's journal entries often cover blocks of time without distinguishing exact dates.

152 New Guinea was under Australian government control, until 1975, when it became the independent country of Papua New Guinea.

a patrol officer[153] and served in that physically fatiguing work for six years. Providentially, Rick was a new believer, having brought himself to faith in Christ by simply reading the New Testament. He once tried to get a Catholic priest to baptize him, but when he insisted on immersion, he was told that "Catholics don't do it that way."[154] However, Rick's recent Christian conversion, along with his patrol[155] work among remote New Guinea villagers, convinced him of the need for stout, pioneering men for the mission.

The crossing of paths in Port Moresby was not viewed by Joe and Rick as mere coincidence, but rather as a divine convergence of their separate journeys and part of the Lord's evangelistic purpose for New Guinea. One afternoon they sat on a hill overlooking the city and pledged that together they would soon extend the gospel to the furthest flung interior tribes they could find.

Joe quickly recognized enormous potential in Rick's experience and knowledge of the local people and languages. Once Rick explained that the highest concentration of unreached tribes was located in the rough and rugged highlands region, Joe secured an Air Nuigini flight to the city of Lae to concentrate his research from there.

Lae was a coastal city of 36,000 people, strategically situated on the Huon Gulf in Morobe Province. It was both a major port city and,

---

153 Patrol officers were often based in remote campsites consisting of bush huts and frequent privations, hardship and danger. Their work included the supervision of building grass airstrips and arduous treks through jungle and mountain terrain to carry out police and magisterial duties, such as gathering data for population census, collecting taxes, and settling tribal disputes.

154 Larry Voyles "Notes and Reminisces" (2012).

155 Bush-walking patrols lasted as long as three months and were mostly without communication with the outside world. All food, sleeping gear, medical supplies, and paperwork had to be hand carried. The patrol officer was accompanied by local native carriers and policemen, trained by the officer and paid by the Australian government. Excerpts adapted from "Australian Patrol Officers (Kiaps) in the TPNG (Territory of Papua New Guinea)", by Senator the Hon. John Faulkner, Special Minister of State, pages 6-7, November 8, 2008.

more importantly, for Joe's spiritual interest in the highlands people, located at the eastern end of the *Highlands Highway*.[156]

In the early 1970s, the Highlands Highway was an 800 mile-long, bone-crushing, thief-thick, land-cruiser killing, glorified gravel road which led into the belly of the New Guinea highlands. There were many ways to die on the Highlands Highway which was less than two lanes wide in many places. Head-on collisions with drunken drivers or suicidal truckers were the frequent, close-call, occupational hazards of road travel. But one could just as easily slide off or be forced over a thousand foot-high precipice, or be road-blocked, robbed, or raped by armed and violent criminals. Many have suffered these horrors and I've experienced a few of them myself.[157] (But this is Joe's story, not mine. Although he was driving the first time I had the strong inclination to surrender my wallet to road thieves!)

Joe's first foray into the highlands was a journey into the Stone Age. He experienced firsthand the myriads of exotic languages, small town settlements, and tribal village people still living and dying with little or no gospel access. Joe breathlessly scribbled out a quick note and wired it to his supporters:

> I have been traveling in (Papua) New Guinea looking for a place to begin our work for Christ. Lae, in the northeast, looks like a good place for a base of operations, so we will move there in the near future. New Guinea abounds with gospel opportunities. Brethren, let us move into this field without delay. – Joe Cannon in New Guinea[158]

---

156   A so-called "highway" only because it was the only road into the interior.

157   I've been road-blocked and robbed, slapped around, and had my side window blown out with a shotgun. I've also driven through bow and arrow tribal fights in Enga Province where warriors on both sides of the road would cease fire, as I passed through, but then continue fighting once I was safely through.

158   Excerpt from a two-paragraph article entitled "New Guinea – A Last Frontier" torn out of a Christian newspaper, the *Christian Observer*, dated in early 1971.

LOVE AND HATE OF MONEY

This might be a good place to describe Joe's ongoing frustration with the use of money. For Joe, money was a tool to be best leveraged for Kingdom advance. He did not have much patience for the human tendency to fearfully squirrel away resources in a hole somewhere.[159] The western view of saving up money for a rainy day was not one that Joe embraced.

When Joe and Rosa Belle moved to Papua New Guinea, it was mutually agreed that the Orient Street Church in Stamford, Texas, would serve as the sponsoring congregation that should send and oversee them in this new work.[160] As Joe neared his 60s in the middle 1980s, the elders recognized that he was getting along in years without any kind of retirement plan. A.D. Smith tells the tale of this classic Joe Cannon episode:[161]

> The church leadership began to withhold 10% of Joe and RB's support for their eventual retirement needs, which seemed to be a good and responsible thing to do. But they didn't tell Joe about it. Somehow he found out and called me from New Guinea, mad as a hornet. He huffed, "They're withholding my money!" He ranted on, "The Lord's going to take care of me when I get too old. I'm not going to retire; I'm going to die in the saddle!"
>
> I tried to reason with him. "Joe, this is a good thing. You're going to need this someday." But Joe insisted. "The Lord will take care of me! If I die on the mission field, fine, bury me on

---

159   Matthew 25:18, 24-29.

160   The Fern Ave Church of Christ (Toronto) faithfully served as Joe and RB's overseeing congregation for the entirety of their twenty-four years of gospel work in Japan and Okinawa.

161   Taped interview (2012) with A.D. Smith, previously an elder with the Walnut Church of Christ in Texarkana, Texas, one of Joe's dearest friends. This is not a direct quote and is edited for brevity. The story is entirely his.

the spot. The Lord will know where to find me!" That is the way the man thought! He never worried about tomorrow.

When Joe learned of the "plot" to secure funds for his retirement he was livid! As a young missionary, I remember his red-faced ranting about it. But understand Joe's perspective: this happened just as the gospel was beginning to take hold upon many remote regions of the New Guinea highlands. Joe was in constant fundraising mode to fuel his dreams of planting churches far and wide throughout the country, and he was in no mood to worry about end of life matters.

JOE WAS SINGULARLY HARD-WIRED, HEART AND SOUL,
FOR THE ADVANCE OF JESUS' NAME.

I am not certain of the details, but he somehow finagled the money from that account for immediate use. Once Joe got his hands on the money, he immediately put it into the New Guinea work. While he was at it, he also cashed out his own life insurance policy and pitched that into the ministry pot as well! Joe categorically detested any hint of retirement notions, even when good brothers tried to put it aside for his own retirement. Joe and Rosa Belle joyfully "mortgaged" their future for the gospel and boasted in the Lord that they had never gone *significantly* hungry. Joe often quipped, "As long as the sparrows eat, we eat. When God quits feeding the sparrows, missionaries will become extinct."

Trusting in God for financial backing and fueled by the exhilaration of being in front-line gospel situations, a few weeks after his New Guinea recon Joe described meeting first friends and recognizing tangible leadings of the Lord with his every step:

> To be in a strange situation and walk into the unknown, step by step, and experience the Lord opening every door for you is thrilling indeed . . . I found an ideal location in the western part of the city (Lae). Two houses on five acres of bush land, through which a small stream flows. What should I do? Action was called for, so I took an option on this $29,000

property . . . The task is tremendous and the journey begins with the first step![162]

Joe's first step was to seal the deal with a personal $10,000 "hot" check and speed home to raise money to cover the commitment.

En route to the states for a brief fundraising tour, Joe stopped over in the Philippines to preach a series of meetings. After he eagerly explained the New Guinea mission, he was joyfully shocked by the generosity of the Filipino brethren who presented him with a gift of $924, which allowed him to travel to Okinawa debt-free in regard to his flight and travel expenses.

Joe and RB at their house in Lae, (1971)

In his beloved Okinawa, Joe passionately challenged the church with the spiritual destitution and lack of gospel access in New Guinea. He was elated by the response of the Ojana congregation when the elders, including his friend and Camp Sosu prayer partner, Flint Garrison, immediately pledged the needed amount for the down payment on the house and property in Lae:

> They gave me $1,000 on the spot, then one week later, following a presentation on our gospel dreams for New Guinea, they took an offering and gave us $1,600 more! What a lovely, shocking experience that was! The Lord is with us, and with brethren like this behind us, we cannot fail.[163]

Several weeks later, Joe reported again, this time, from Japan:

> I have presented the New Guinea mission 15 times. Churches in Okinawa, Tokyo, and Ibaraki have already promised

---

162 Joe Cannon newsletter, "New Guinea Mission: To the Land of the Last Unknown," early 1971.

163 Joe Cannon newsletter, "New Guinea Mission," February, 1971.

monthly support for this outreach. Two Japanese preachers want to enter the New Guinea field themselves . . . The church in Hitachi will handle funds raised from Japan for the New Guinea work and will also help support any workers that go out from there.[164]

One of the great thrills for Joe and Rosa Belle in their missionary lives was the enthusiastic way Japanese and Okinawan churches, their children in faith, responded to the New Guinea mission, with both money and missionaries for the work.

From Japan, it was onward to the United States and Canada. Apparently, Joe was already legendary in some quarters of North America for flexing radical financial faith whenever he thought aggressive gospel advance warranted it.

JOE BELIEVED THAT LACK OF MONEY SHOULD NEVER SLOW THE WORK OF THE GOSPEL, AND HE EXEMPLIFIED TRUSTING THAT IT WOULDN'T.

As Joe made the quick swing through stateside and Canadian churches with his vision for New Guinea, he encountered various levels of pushback. Everyone was thrilled at the spread of the gospel through Joe and RB's labors, however, some were put off by his aggressive pleas for the money to do the work.

If people were irritated because they thought he *expected* them to finance the ministry, they were right. Joe could get irritated as well! He never viewed himself as a financial beggar but rather as a gospel ambassador, sent on a Great Commission that required massive resources. He was not squeamish in asking for those resources. Joe reasoned that if he and Rosa Belle were willing to joyfully and eagerly plunge their family, repeatedly into the depths of spiritual darkness on gospel rescue missions around the world, the brethren should at least finance the journey.

---

164   Joe Cannon newsletter, "New Guinea Mission: Japanese Churches Respond," March, 1971.

In research for this book, I came across an interesting phrase several times in Joe's writings, as early as the late 1940s. He wrote about those who "took blood from us." I did not understand what he meant until I read a thank you letter from Joe to a "Brother Lovelady."[165] Apparently, Mr. Lovelady had sent financial support to the Cannons, but a hang-up with international mail delivery had delayed its arrival. Joe was much relieved when the check finally arrived in "a close shave," as he called it, just in time to meet some undisclosed need. But then he added these revealing sentences:

> Our financial support is widely scattered which makes it difficult to keep up with. Every now and then, someone "draws blood from us" and it hurts. I hope you will stay with us until '64 (next furlough).

Joe took it personally when financial supporters dropped them without warning. He considered it to be desertion and likened it to "blood-letting!"[166]

The Cannons were incredibly gracious and grateful for faithful ministry partners, and they did not expect financial contributors to remain with them forever. However, Joe resented the shabby treatment that missionaries sometimes experienced. Even more important than the financial support itself, Joe never understood the seeming fickleness of supporters who did not grasp the eternal urgency of getting the gospel to unreached peoples. Money for the Great Commission was in the pockets, but it seemed not to squeeze very well through the heart.

A Christian newspaper article described Joe's humorous demeanor as he traveled around various congregations in the States and Canada:

---

165   Dated December 23, 1961, interestingly just one week after the accidental death of Ivy Rose in Okinawa.

166   In Joe's defense, consider the context. Prior to the early 1980s, foreign missionaries relied on receiving support checks through the postal service until wire transfers became more common. "Direct deposit" wasn't even in our vocabulary. When support was sent mistakenly by sea-mail instead of air mail, it could sometimes be delayed for weeks. Sometimes it never arrived at all. Indeed, it felt like "blood-letting."

After completing his presentations, Mr. Cannon encourages questions. Sometimes he injects a bit of humor and wit. Once, after he gave a report to a group of elders and deacons [expressing the financial need], there was a quiet lull during the question period. Finally, Mr. Cannon broke the silence by retorting, "Go ahead and shoot me! I'm a Cannon! I've been shot before!"[167]

By the time Joe arrived in Texas, it came as no surprise to R.C. (Cliff) Cobb to learn that Joe had written a personal check to secure the New Guinea property. Cliff would often chide Joe, privately, that he really should not "fly off" and make financial commitments without talking to anybody first. At the same time, Cliff understood Joe's single-minded concern for lost souls and the decades of his risking life and limb in order to get them under the gospel. Cliff, the Orient Street Church of Christ in Stamford, Texas, and many others had already experienced this sort of financial "chutzpah" from Joe's earlier work in Japan and Okinawa. Though sometimes chafed by Joe's financial frolics, they highly esteemed him because of the way he and Rosa Belle frequently put their bodies in perilous places for the gospel. When Joe passionately pled for finances to do their work, it seemed reasonable to their supporters. How could they not finance someone who was willing to go anywhere, do anything, and put up with all sorts of things "so that the spread of the gospel would not be hindered?"[168]

Brother Cobb talked the Texas congregation into mortgaging their building and borrowing the money to "finish off" the purchase of the New Guinea property. In classic Joe Cannon jubilance, he gushed:

> A special thanks to the Orient Street Church of Stamford, Texas for sticking their necks out to borrow fifteen thousand dollars. The Lord will make them happy because of this![169]

---

167 *Christian Observer, Vol. 4, No. 8,* June 1971, Memphis, TN.

168 1 Corinthians 9:12, J.B. Phillips, "The New Testament in Modern English," 1962 edition, Harper Collins.

169 News from New Guinea Report, September 22, 1971.

Mr. Cobb was heard to say, more than once over the years, "Joe Cannon will be the death of me!" But it was always whispered with a chuckle, a grin and teary eyes that conveyed his admiration of a man who had the spiritual and physical guts to do what he did for the advance of Jesus' name.[170]

Joe spoke more than 65 times throughout Canada and the states of Tennessee, Arkansas, Oklahoma, and Texas, promoting their hopes for gospel success in New Guinea. With fundraising finally behind them, Joe and Rosa Belle returned to Okinawa for a few weeks to sort, pack, and ship their necessary belongings to New Guinea.

One week before the Cannon departure, Joe wrote a poignant, final correspondence from Okinawa to his supporters in North America:[171]

> We are now spending our last week on Okinawa. For nine years we have served our Lord here and now, as the time of our departure approaches, we feel sad. We have sold our house and our family has been reduced from six to three.

> We are parting from good friends we love. Okinawa and its people and our days have been happy ones. We shall never forget our brethren here.

> God has given us some fruit in this land, but we must follow his leading. Our days were not always bright as there are two graves we leave behind, my mother's and our little Ivy Rose's.

On August 13, 1971, reminiscent of the Apostle Paul's sendoff from the Ephesian believers,[172] the Cannon family, minus Eileen who was

---

170 I met Mr. Cobb in the highlands outpost of Mt. Hagen in 1981. He visited New Guinea and saw with his own eyes what Joe's ragged-edged faith (and his own) had accomplished for the speedy spread of Jesus' name.

171 August 5, 1971.

172 Acts 20:1.

now married and Joey and Debbie who remained stateside for college, departed the Naha International Airport, en route for New Guinea. Many Okinawan brethren, with an exultant *sayonara* (for a while), sent them into their next venture for Christ.

FIRST THINGS FIRST

The city of Lae is a sultry sweathouse during the dry season. Temperatures can soar into the low 100s only briefly lowered, but 90% humidified, by rainy season downpours of more than 200 inches per year. Joe and RB were sucker-punched by the sudden swoosh of equatorial heat as they stepped onto the Air Nuigini jet-way ladder. No one waited to welcome them.

It was August 19, 1971, their first day on mission for Christ in New Guinea, and Joe and Rosa Belle were starting from scratch. With three children in tow, their first assignment was to rent a car, secure their house key, rent a post office box, and purchase basic food stuffs. When they tracked down their new home on the edge of town, they found that three squatter families had taken up residence in the vacant house, making it a well-lived-in mess. While Greg, Leonard, and Robin eagerly explored the five-acre property, Joe and Rosa Belle gently evicted[173] the occupants and proceeded to scrub the floors and walls, repair broken window panes, dump trash, and endlessly stomp roaches and spray mosquitoes.

New Guinea townships get raucous when the sun goes down, especially for weary, jet-lagged missionaries. Newcomers quickly learned that the zaniest sounds of the night were not the flapping wings of fruit bats, croaking bullfrogs, or even the drunken parties in the neighborhood. The most annoying jungle jingles were the shrieking insects that provoked the five Cannons to plug their ears with wads of toilet paper. The New Guinea newbies boiled drinking water until they could

---

173 Though the squatters had no legal rights, Joe wisely and thoughtfully arranged for a water tank to be delivered and installed on the back portion of the property for the people he removed from their house.

trust it and then swatted and sweated through the first night without electricity and with only exhausting, head-bobbing bits of sleep.

The northernmost islands of Papua New Guinea lie just beneath the equator. No more dress shirts and neckties for Joe in that tropic climate! Male expatriates in the coastal cities often wore an Australian-style ensemble of light-colored, short-sleeved safari suits with short pants and knee socks. Joe added a "Gilligan-style" bucket hat for sun protection. Later he settled into a more North American style of shorts, t-shirts, and tennis shoes. On a rare evening out to dinner at the Red Rose Chinese restaurant, a colorful Filipino shirt and slacks served as formal wear. Expat women wore cotton short-sleeved dresses and loafers or tennis shoes.

One of the items on Joe's immediate to-do list was to secure the new four-wheel drive Toyota Land Cruiser he had purchased from Japan and had shipped to Lae. During these first days in New Guinea, Joe also acquired a Morris Mini-Moke. This was essentially a tin-sled go-cart with a rag top. Think of it as a low-rider golf cart with a loud engine. However, it was New Guinea road legal and could seat two people easily, four people awkwardly, and five people sometimes (as long as Rosa Belle didn't know about it). The Mini-Moke became a common sight for more than a decade, hauling around town like the Flintstones, usually with one of the single missionaries at the helm. I happen to know that one young missionary sometimes strapped a surfboard on top of it and made his way to the beach side of the Lae airstrip.[174]

During the earliest days of learning life in New Guinea, the Cannon clan provided good entertainment for the locals. Passers-by gawked as they walked by the houseful of strange-looking white skins. Some of these curious visitors became Joe and RB's first New Guinea friends, including Joss Aiep and Ate (Simon) Gerel who were coaxed into their home for cold drinks and cookies.

Joe and Joss became best buddies and were an unusual twosome. Joe was tall, lean, and pale white in contrast to Joss' short, stout stat-

---

174 That would be me, but it was solely for evangelistic purposes. I had an Australian surfing buddy (John Moore) who became a believer in Christ, married one of our single missionaries (Cami Box) and still continues in ministry today.

ure and bushy black hair and skin. They were all the more entertaining when they traipsed around the property hand in hand![175]

Joss quickly became Joe's tutor in the Melanesian Pidgin[176] language. Pidgin, "tok pisin" as it's known in-country, is the nationally recognized lingua-franca[177] of Papua New Guinea (PNG). Pidgin developed in the early 1800s as a result of increased travel and economic activity between Melanesians and Europeans. The devastating effects of World War II upon New Guinea accelerated its widespread use. Pidgin, a conglomer-

Joss Aiep, first PNG convert

ate of several world languages including English, German, French, and Dutch, is also influenced by many of the island's 800-plus tribal languages.

As Joss instructed Joe in language and culture, the walls in the Cannon house were soon plastered with posters of Pidgin words for Joe and RB's review. But Joe's most effective language acquisition occurred while on hunting and hiking trips. Joe had a handy 12-gauge shotgun that intrigued Joss. Stalking exotic birds, such as cockatoos and various species of parrots and birds of paradise, was a pastime they both enjoyed. But Joss was equally interested in cutting black palm from the jungle to craft bows and arrows to sell to the tourists in Lae.

During these bush excursions, Joe was always on the lookout to capture animals for the personal zoo that he stocked behind their house.

---

175 Holding hands is what male friends in PNG often do. It is a gesture of friendly affection and companionship.

176 Tok Pisin is one of the three national languages of PNG, including Motu and English.

177 A language people use to communicate when they have different first languages; a trade language.

A prominent 8 by 16-foot wire cage sat outside RB's kitchen window. She often stood at her sink talking to her pet bird, a Black-Capped Lorikeet named Turu. When it was especially hot outside, RB sprayed Turu with cool water from the sink. Sometimes Turu was brought inside the house so he could fly free for a while. Joe loved to drink icy Cokes right out of the freezer. Turu would swoop in for a landing and latch onto the cold bottle, hugging it with his wings close to his chest. Joe happily shared his cokes with Turu and joked about how the bird was sure "lovin'" that Coke bottle![178]

Rosa Belle also had a dog named Honey Girl. Turu could closely mimic Rosa Belle's voice and Joe's whistling and constantly antagonized the dog with his tricks. Once Turu called out to Honey Girl with Joe's imitated whistle and she came racing around the back corner of the house, only to realize that Turu had fooled her again. Honey Girl ambled away with a disgusted look on her face![179] When Honey Girl was old, one of the New Guinea nationals suggested that he assist Joe by putting her "out of her misery." Joe agreed. He later learned Honey Girl had been kindly relieved of her suffering, but also became a meaty meal for the helpful brother's family![180]

Joe's and RB's menagerie included at various times: two tree kangaroos, several opossums, Eclectus Parrots, a Sulphur-crested Cockatoo, a Green Tree Python, several other species of larger pythons, and the ever-popular eight-foot-long crocodile that was isolated and well secured in a cement pond with a heavy wire fence. People came from far and wide to see Joe's zoo.

One afternoon a Lutheran pastor came to complain that Joe, in his evangelistic efforts, was stealing his "sheep." In the course of the conversation, Joe showed him the animals and asked if he knew how his crocodile had gotten so big. Then Joe smiled and

---

178 Larry Voyles, personal notes.

179 Ruth Niland's recollection during a 2011 interview.

180 Interview with Robin Cannon, April 25, 2014.

jokingly said, "Because I feed him Lutherans!" Yet another way Joe could disarm an uncomfortable conversation.

These bush adventures and animal escapades provided innumerable, ready-made occasions to stretch the margins of Joe's and RB's Pidgin vocabulary. As Joe's language skills improved, he began to give the gospel to Joss who then became their first New Guinea convert.

By this time, Rick Niland had relocated to Lae. Rick's intent was to work closely with the Cannons in their highlands church planting efforts. But first Joe detoured him through Lubbock, Texas, to acquire some biblical training at the Sunset School of Preaching.

SEAT-OF-THE-PANTS STRATEGY

Joe's evangelistic approach was to form friendships with as many locals as possible and search for ways to love Christ and the gospel into them. The how and how not's of doing that in New Guinea were acquired the hard way through a tough few years of learning the linguistic and cultural "rules of the rainforest."

Joe and RB simply started where they were, utilized what they had, and applied what they thought they knew. Years earlier, while still in college, they had resolved to preach Christ to the "poorest of the poor," and the Lord had settled them in the middle of cave-dwelling refugees in post-war Japan. Nearly a quarter-century later, it's fascinating to see how the Lord clearly directed Joe's purchase of the Lae property, set squarely on the edge of a dilapidated squatter settlement. If they wanted to preach the gospel to the poor, the Lord surely put them in the right place, and they vigorously stepped into the squalor. Their backyard friends became their initial priority. The squatter commune was populated by several hundred poverty-stricken highlanders from a dozen diverse tribal cultures who had migrated to Lae looking for jobs or simply to live near their *wantoks*.[181]

---

181   *Wantok* is a Pidgin word for a fellow tribe member; one who speaks a common heart language. *Wantok* has also come to include anyone who is considered to be a close friend.

Highland tribes are more rambunctious and shorter-fused than tribes in the lowlands cultures. When a bunch of hot-headed highlanders, who may already have a history of bad blood with one another, are crammed[182] into close proximity and tight living conditions, the resulting atmosphere teeters on the edge of explosion. Add alcohol, theft, promiscuity, gambling, and heaps of idle time into the cultural mix, and there was ample fuel for volatile eruptions.

Despite surrounding conditions, Joe and RB were flexible and a lot of fun to be with. They engaged the people with lively conversation. Rosa Belle's reserved bashfulness was Joe's perfect counterbalance as he loudly entertained the children with boisterous bantering. They quickly conquered the suspicions of their backyard neighbors and further earned their trust by providing *pasim sua*[183] clinics. Soon hundreds of people were stopping by the house to get their wounds bandaged or hitch the occasional ride to the hospital for more serious accidents. In a community rife with routine drunkenness, fist fights, and marital spats, there were many mishaps. Joe was often recruited to referee these late-night disturbances.

One incident resulted in fisticuffs in the Cannon's front yard. Joe had assisted a woman with a quick get-away from her violent husband, only to be jumped by a group of Chimbu roughnecks. Joss, who was a Wabag[184] highlander himself jumped into the fray with Joe and "deposited them one by one into a nearby ditch."[185]

The Lae police offered to arrest the instigator, but Joe declined to press charges. Instead, he reasoned, "If the highlanders are going to drink beer and carouse on our property, then I'm going to use their

---

182 No one forced them to live in these settlements. Lack of finances exacerbated these situations and is a common problem associated with rapid urbanization.

183 Pidgin words roughly translated "bind up sores," but understood to be a basic medical clinic.

184 Wabag is a small highlands outpost and the provincial capital of Enga Province.

185 Joseph L. Cannon, *The Experiences of a New Guinea Pig (1974)*, pages 41, Hall Publishing House, Texarkana, TX.

shenanigans for my own gospel advantage." As leader of a street gang in his younger days, Joe understood something about hoodlums and befriended the trouble makers. On another occasion, Joe and RB were giving refuge to a battered wife. The unruly husband showed up at the door and got abusive with Joe. The former Rideau Rat laid him out with a single fist thump to the side of his skull![186]

Eventually, Joe mail-ordered a set of handcuffs from Australia for his evangelistic purposes. Whenever he found himself in the middle of drunken brawlers who wanted to fight, he put them in a headlock (he was big enough to do it), handcuffed them if necessary, and deposited them at the police station for an overnight stay. The next morning he bailed them out and brought them home where RB cooked up a hearty breakfast while he preached the gospel to them.

JESUS AND JOE DRIED OUT MORE THAN ONE RABBLE-ROUSING DRUNKARD WHO FOUND THEIR WAY TO CHRIST THROUGH THE CANNON'S "RECKLESS" HOSPITALITY.

The Cannon's white frame house became a well-known hangout and mini-medical treatment center that attracted a steady stream of patients. As the *pasim sua* clinics grew larger, those with other problems such as malaria, scabies, and various body aches and muscle strains would form long lines to wait their turn. Occasionally women whose husbands beat them up came seeking help or protection. Sometimes it was the men who showed up with cracked heads and body lacerations. Flying projectiles hurled by angry wives were a frequent cause of male discomfort in the settlement!

During each clinic day Joe ordered a time out and he or Rick told Bible stories to the patients, weaving in gospel truths along the way. Afterwards the clinic resumed for a few hours longer. This was the weekly approach that provided countless opportunities to demonstrate love for people and for the gospel of Christ, both entirely free of charge and doled out with careful compassion. Frequent visitors quickly real-

---

186 David Berim, a PNG highlander and brother in Christ, told me this story in Mt. Hagen in 2011.

ized that the missionaries were even more interested in patching their shredded souls than repairing their tattered torsos.

TWO DOLLAR RECONCILIATION

Tanike's late-night knock on the front door alerted Joe that Jak and a few of the brothers were getting drunk on the church property. Greatly disappointed, Joe went and broke up the party. Once sobered up, Jak was still angry that Tanike had reported his beer drinking to Joe. He found Tanike and punched him in the head, knocking him into the bushes. Joe happened to be standing nearby and responded with a hard smack to the side of Jak's head. Stunned, but unhurt, Jak walked away rubbing his head.

Joe was immediately ashamed of having punched Jak. Knowing the New Guinea custom of paying compensation for any violence done to another person, Joe went to Jak, apologized and gave him two dollars. Jak then reflected upon his own sin against Tanike and went

to find him. "I have wronged you, my Christian brother," he said and gave him the two dollars. Tanike then went to Joe's house and gave him the two dollars as a show of gratitude for having stood up for him against Jak. The two dollars went full circle and so did the forgiveness that was extended one to another. Joe remarked later, "I have never had the experience of *not* being

Tanike Pimbin

forgiven by Papua New Guineans when I apologized and followed their customs. They understand what the gospel means in brotherly relationships. For my part, I had to travel a long way to learn how to forgive and be forgiven by my New Guinea brothers."

The missionaries learned to live out the gospel alongside their New Guinea friends. Soon there was a small group of believers meeting on Sundays at Rick's house, which was just a few hundred feet from the Cannon's. As the congregation grew, the internal walls were removed and the roof was extended over open air to create a meeting place that would accommodate more than 100 people.

Joe gladly shared preaching opportunities with new missionaries, stateside visitors, and students in the School of Life. Occasionally though, Joe intervened when the messages went awry. On one memorable occasion, a brother from the Southern Highlands was preaching. He was troubled by a recent plague of locusts that was causing havoc with crops in the Markham Valley. As he meandered into predicting the Second Coming of Christ based upon this local event, Joe walked politely to the platform and asked him to sit down while he mopped up the theological mess.

The embryonic group of believers represented a hodge-podge of tribes with widely divergent linguistic and cultural variances. The mutually understood language was Pidgin, but in the early 1970s, newly arriving villagers from the remotest places struggled to understand it.

Despite the ethno-linguistic challenges, intentional efforts were made to create an environment that was intelligible to as many people as possible. As the church developed, Wednesday evenings became multi-lingual gatherings. Believers from the various language groups were invited to sing, give testimony, or preach in their own *tok ples*[187] languages. Paraphrased translation into Pidgin was provided, but rather than insisting on word-for-word interpretation, the greater intent was to enjoy joint celebration of the Lord with believers from different ethnicities. It became a small slice of heaven[188] for the congregation to experience Christ being praised in so many different languages.[189] Joe or Rick would preach and teach Bible classes while RB taught literacy

---

187   *Tok ples* is Pidgin for "mother tongue."

188   Revelation 5:9-10; 7:9-10.

189   Some of the languages spoken in the Lae congregation were those of the Timbe, Chimbu, Tami, Waria, Menyamya, Wabag, Melpa, and Gumine peoples.

to those who couldn't read and mentored women in the everyday issues of marriage, child care, and healthier hygienic practices for their families. In many ways, this was a PNG implementation of the "all things . . . to all people . . . through all means . . . so that some will be saved"[190] methodology that they previously used in Japan and Okinawa.

After nearly five months in country, by the end of 1971, Joe struggled through his first efforts in Pidgin preaching.[191] He described it this way:

> For the past five Sundays I have preached in Pidgin at a Sunday evening meeting we started up the hill behind our place. We carry kerosene lamps to a place called "One Mile" and 50-90 people gather to hear the gospel. I read the first three sermons, but the last two I was able to preach from an outline. Pity the audience and pity my poor head but I am happy to preach . . . I hope for good results, but it is God "that gives the increase."

By 1972 the fast-growing missionary team in Lae expanded to include Joe and Rosa Belle Cannon, Rick Niland, Duane and Carol Morgan, the Gary Hyer family, and the newly arrived Reg and Ruth Coles (who later pioneered the gospel in the Papuan Waria region). The Morgan and Hyer families arrived in Port Moresby (independently of Joe and RB) from a church in Tennessee and decided to join forces and work together in Lae. In quick succession, Lorna Fairley and David and Karen Lock joined the team in 1974.[192]

Apparently there were some missiological differences from the beginning as to how to proceed in the work. Duane and Gary were younger guys with strong personalities who had innovative ideas that didn't always gel with Joe's more traditional approach to mission. Before long, Duane and Gary relocated to the smaller town of Goroka in the Eastern Highlands to forge a ministry from there. Joe resisted the notion that

---

190   I Corinthians 9:22.

191   Joe Cannon, New Guinea Newsletter, December 1, 1971.

192   The timeline for new missionary arrivals comes from *Walking in Yesterday*, page 12, 1985.

there was harmful "division" and only said there was mutual agreement to work in separate locations. Rick Niland, who knew and worked with both Duane and Joe commented,[193] "Duane was young and difficult to work with, and we all know that Joe was sometimes hard to work with as well." Following some years in Goroka, Duane Morgan relocated to Papua, Indonesia,[194] and continues to minister there. Happily, as we will see in a later chapter, Joe and Duane were reunited years later in a very satisfying and fruitful ministry together in Indonesia.

A consistent theme began to emerge as I gathered insights from PNG believers for *Hard Fighting Soldier*. When asked for a personal story that described their friendship with Joe, several men became visibly emotional. One afternoon in 2011, Tanike Pimbin and I were sitting on the dirt with our backs propped up against the small church building in Mt. Hagen. Tanike unashamedly wept as he told me about his lifelong struggle with particular sinful behaviors. He repeated the words *pundaun kirap* which is Pidgin for "fall down and get up." As a new believer, and even as an older one, Tanike honestly confessed how he frequently "fell into sin." However, Joe always helped him to "get up." Over and over again. *Pundaun kirap. Pundaun kirap.* Joe never wavered in his encouragement, even through Tanike's long years of struggle with some of the same sins. Because Joe never gave up on him in his failures, Tanike came to understand at a deep level the grace and love of Christ for him in the gospel, and that Jesus does not leave him either.

GOSPEL PATROLS

Joe was antsy to spread his missionary wings more widely into the highlands regions. As the number of believers increased in the settlement so did the requests for Joe to visit their home villages.

---

193   Rick Niland, personal interview in Brisbane, Australia, 2011.

194   Formerly known as Dutch New Guinea and Irian Jaya.

Rarely refusing an invitation, Joe made verbal commitments to people in at least six highland provinces.[195]

Joe in the New Guinea highlands

Morobe province, where Lae serves as the capital city, is not usually included in "highlands" discussions. However, Morobe is renowned for some of the most severe mountain ranges of PNG, including Menyamya and the Sarawagued Mountains. Similarly, the Western and Sandaun provinces are home to the Star Mountains with peaks in excess of 12,000 feet. Mt. Wilhelm, at 14,793 feet, is the highest of the mountains, and some of the major mountain summits remain unnamed on many maps. It was (and is) in these treacherous elevations where the hardest to reach tribes still reside. It requires bountiful amounts of physical and spiritual bravery, raw faith, perseverance, and unusual creativity to get to these farthest-flung peoples. Gospel advance might

River baptism

be via four-wheel drive vehicles, PMV[196] trucks, ships, canoes, chartered airplanes, or helicopters[197] but always with a hefty overdose of tough bush walking. Spearheading the gospel to the interior usually entails a resourceful combination of at least two or three of these modes of transport.

---

195 Morobe, Eastern Highlands, Chimbu, Western Highlands, Southern Highlands, and Enga.

196 A public motor vehicle might be a pick-up truck, a huge flat-bed company truck where you toss your gear and self on top of whatever cargo is being hauled (vegetables, coffee, tobacco) or a 40 passenger truck with tarp tops, tightly packed with people and personal cargo including pigs, chickens, birds, dogs or snakes.

197 We didn't usually plan for helicopters as they are too expensive to charter. If one was on a helicopter, it was most likely a medical evacuation en route to a hospital!

Utilizing Rick Niland's experience as a government patrol officer, Joe referred to these gospel ventures as "patrols." Contact Patrols, Preaching Patrols, Encouragement Patrols . . . memorable experiences are quickly amassed on these out-of-the-way bush excursions.

THE RIOT ACT

Simon Gerel was among the first dozen converts. He promptly invited himself to escort Joe to his home village among the Sina Sina people in Chimbu province. Upon arrival, Joe was greeted with immediate hostility. Loudmouthed village leaders surrounded him, demanding to know why he was in their village uninvited.

"Simon invited me," Joe objected.[198]

"What are you doing here?"

"I came to preach Jesus."

"Who sent you?" they asked.

"Jesus!" Joe replied.

"We don't want you here!" they shouted.

"OK. You don't have to listen."

The confrontation escalated into a full-scale riot. Nearly 400 shouting villagers yelled for Joe to leave or be beaten up. But Joe stood his ground. A wild-looking warrior pushed his way through the crowd and threatened Joe with a stone axe. "Do you see this axe? If you're still here in the morning, I'm going to *give* it to you!" (Obviously not as a gift!)

---

198 Adapted from Joe's unpublished book, *The Heart of a Missionary*, chapter XXVII, "Kill Me First!", page 61.

Village evangelism

The animated shouting match was repeated in the morning with all the village leaders gathered and a few hundred people milling around to watch the festivities. Joe sauntered into the middle of the crowd, making jokes, laughing, and giving the people little snippets of the gospel.

The antagonist watched from the top of a hill, furiously brandishing his axe and spitting out threats. With a shrieking war cry, he charged down on Joe with his axe swinging! Villagers scattered out of the way. Joe wrote later, "I didn't tremble a bit. I was frozen on the spot!" At the last moment a man dashed out of the crowd and flung himself in front of Joe, shielding him from the whirling axe head. He grabbed the machete man around the waist and dragged him to the ground. It was Joe's friend Simon shouting, "Kill me first! Joe is my brother. Kill me first!"

The man lowered his axe and the crisis was over. However, Joe was put on village trial in their tribal council and was further threatened if he refused to leave. Joe used the opportunity to give the gospel, which only incited them again. The riot began again with loud verbal bullying. Finally wearied from the waste of time, Joe tipped his hat and walked away to continue preaching in the surrounding villages.

Joe's summation was "that no one tried to restrain me further, I went on with my preaching plans. The Lord was with me and today there are many churches in Chimbu, even among the Sina Sina where the riot occurred." Joe concluded, ". . . there is one person I love most of all in that region. He made me his brother and risked his life for me. His name is Simon."

In these same mountains of Chimbu, Joe witnessed wonderful success as he preached the gospel in the village of Gorabeng,[199] and many

---

199 Story related by Robin Cannon, May 2014.

were converted to Christ. The leading men contemplated how they should destroy a large, extremely heavy ancestral stone god that had been passed down through many generations. They asked Joe how they should dispose of it. He simply asked if he could have it as a memento

R & R following a hard day's walk and work in Wabag

to the grace of God that had been shown in Gorabeng. They were happy to be rid of the burden, and Joe kept it the rest of his life. It is now an important part of a collection of artifacts that testify to the advance of the gospel in Chimbu.

SCHOOL OF LIFE / MELANESIAN BIBLE COLLEGE

Two young men, Yusi Miopa and David Isawe, persistently pressed Joe to provide more in-depth Bible teaching. When Rick Niland returned to PNG following his own stint in Bible school, Joe's first assignment was to begin a Pidgin-language Christian school devoted to basic biblical instruction and leadership training.[200]

The kick-off class for the *School of Life (SOL)* was organized in February 1975 with 26 students. Joe Cannon, Ray Lock, David Lock, and Rick Niland taught the courses. (Rick also served as the first principal.)[201] Subsequent principals were Larry Voyles

Joe, School of Life, Lae, PNG

---

200 Information regarding the early years of the School of Life comes from the PNG Team booklet entitled "Walking in Yesterday" (1979). Revised at least twice in 1981 and 1985.

201 The timeline of those serving in leadership of the SOL / MBC is pieced together from "Walking in Yesterday" and e-mail correspondence with Ruth Zimmerman, Jab Mesa and Art Ford.

(1977), Art Ford (1978-1986), Woody Square (1986-1991), Andy Scott (1992), Jon Kerenga (1993-1996), and Jab Mesa (1996-Present).

I had not yet arrived in-country, but knowing the missionaries involved, I can easily imagine the fiery discussions that necessarily took place as the SOL was in the birth canal:

> Joe to Rick Niland: "We need to begin a Bible training school for young men. You can do this!"

> Before Rick answered, Ray Lock (an accountant) asked: "Where do we get the money, Joe?"

> Joe: "We'll get it, don't worry." (Turning back to Rick)

> Joe to Rick: "How soon can you begin the school?"

> Before Rick answered, Ray forcefully reiterated: "JOE! Where will we get the money?"

> Joe: "We'll get it, Ray, don't worry!"

> Ray: "We don't have any money, Joe!"

> Joe: "Let's pray it in and go with what we have until it comes!"

> Rick: "Do you want me to start the school or not?"

> Joe: "Start it!"

> Ray: "We don't have any money!"

And on it would go from there. Joe's approach was always that the Lord *will* provide. Ray, on the other hand, needed to see provision on the front side.

Joe directed Rick to start the school. The money arrived in due time, past-due time for Ray's liking, but it worked out. Actually, as the small team of missionaries pooled their work funds to feed the first batch of students,

Joe jokingly responded: "Praise the Lord! He provided!" Ray grimaced. Rick started the school. And a cord of three strands was not quickly broken.[202]

These brothers loved each other dearly and found ways to accomplish some amazing things together. There were some rough relational waters, but to my knowledge, they never stopped loving or working with one another because of it. In separate interviews with Rick and Ruth Niland and the Ray and Elizabeth Lock (extended) family in 2011,[203] they exchanged stories about Joe and RB with enthusiastic laughter, respect and admiration for the Cannons, and gratefulness to the Lord for their own part in the PNG ministry.

As a second-year missionary in 1978, one of my assignments was to drive Rick's mustard yellow Land Cruiser a few hundred miles into the highlands to "round up" students for the school. When I asked, "Where exactly do I go to find these students?" Joe and Rick gave me the names of a few villages I had previously visited with them. Thankfully, by this time I spoke Pidgin.

Joe to me: "Pray and go boldly. Shake the bushes!"

Me: "What if they're not believers?"

Joe: "Give them the gospel."

Thinking back on it, I was not bothered by the seeming absurdity of the plan. Instead, I was exhilarated by an opportunity to just go boldly with bald-faced faith that Jesus would get me where He wanted me, and He would fill the Land Cruiser with young men of his choosing. Or, He wouldn't provide the people, and I would return to Lae with an empty vehicle. Either way, I was eager to see what the Lord would do.

I prayed and naively drove hundreds of miles into the Eastern Highlands and Chimbu provinces to "recruit" students. A week later, I returned with 16 young men packed elbow to elbow and face to face in the back compartment of the Land Cruiser.

---

202 Ecclesiastes 4:12.

203 Ray Lock went to be with the Lord in 2013.

Most of the highlands highway in those days was a multi-pot-holed, washboard-rutted road.[204] The students had a choice to make. They could keep the side windows open and get caked with road dust or keep them closed (with no air-flow) and suffer a heat stroke. They opted for dusty air flow, and I rapid-fired it for Lae, rattling hard over the chassis-challenging pot holes, single-lane wooden bridges, and slip-sliding around the high mountain S-curves.

A slide window separated the front cabin and the back compartment.[205] After several hours of hard driving, I slid the window open and tossed a couple of stalks of bananas to the boys in the back. Within ten minutes they were pounding on the window begging for mercy! One of the fellows had vomited, which caused a chain reaction with most of the rest of them. We had quite a stinking mess by the time I could find a stream to help them get cleaned up. If I remember correctly, Joe howled with laughter when he heard the story and promoted me to "Dean of Students" for the school year.

The School of Life started with a few grass-thatched huts and some rough-hewn young renegades from highlands villages where Joe had planted a handful of fledgling congregations. As I researched Joe's SOL files, I uncovered an old brochure that described the vision statement for the School of Life. One priority was "to preach the gospel for the conversion of non-Christian students." We did that. If they weren't believers when they arrived, after we gave them the gospel, many believed in Christ and a good number of those carried the gospel into some harsh and hostile places over the next 40 years with some eternally wonderful results.

An early cultural concern was the limited attention span of oral[206] learners. We tried to be culturally careful not to overload lecture hours and to engage the students in plenty of practical work. The result was

---

204 On one highlands driving patrol, I experienced five tire blowouts in less than three days.

205 The students called it a *kalabus*, Pidgin for "prison cell." It even had bars over the windows.

206 Oral learners are not accustomed to learning through long lectures. Training is far more than verbal didactics but should also prioritize the practical doing of what they are hearing, i.e. on-the-job tutoring.

two months in class followed by two months in village situations. Ideally, students were mentored by more mature believers assisting with the physical and spiritual needs of new congregations in remote areas.

By 1984, most of the teaching was done by national men. The School of Life (SOL) was renamed the Melanesian Bible College (MBC) in the late 1980s. More than 60 young men graduated from the SOL during the first nine years. Since then, the Melanesian Bible College has continued to train men for ministry who have served Christ in 16 of the 22 provinces of PNG.[207]

Alongside biblical training for men was a corresponding arts department focused on the needs of women and children, particularly for illiterate[208] believers. The purpose of the Arts Department was to teach Pidgin literacy, train women Bible teachers, and teach the practical skills necessary for them to become faithful wives and mothers. The Arts Department began in 1975 with 15 students in an open area next to the Lae church building. Early teachers were Rosa Belle Cannon, Ruth Niland, Elizabeth Lock, Lois Lock, Bessie Phypers, and Nancy Merritt (who served as Director of the Arts Department until at least 1985).

ASCENDING AIWOMBA[209]

He makes my feet like the feet of a deer; He enables me to stand on the heights. He trains my hands for battle; my arms can bend a bow of bronze.

Psalm 18:33-34

The New Guinea mountaineer does not follow the path of least resistance. Instead of gradually ascending mountain heights, sometimes he

---

207 Art Ford (e-mail correspondence), May 14, 2014.

208 "Pre-literate" may be more accurate. New Guinea tribespeople were not historically literate as their languages had never been reduced to written forms. The first language most nationals learned to read and write was Pidgin.

209 Edited from *The Heart of the Missionary,* Joe Cannon, (Self-published, 1994, New Zealand), Chapter XXII, "Ascending the Heights," pages 29-30.

just goes straight up. It was our third day of climbing the Menyamya Mountains, and it was raining. Small rivers of rushing water swept down the footpaths threatening to knock us off of our feet. We were slipping and sliding on our backsides and shivering from the wet cold of the tropical mountains. Exhaustion, aches, pains . . . *when will we ever get there?* As we leveled off onto the summit shelf and trudged across it, we got a beautiful glimpse down into the Aiwomba valley. Suddenly, we remembered why we were there. We saw columns of smoke rising from dozens of thatch-roofed huts. It was as if the smoke was inviting us to the warmth of the village fires and beckoning us to preach the gospel where it had never been preached before. Suddenly, the toils of the rugged trails were forgotten as the nearly naked villagers, with pig tusks through their noses, grass skirts, and beaten bark capes as their only clothing, crowded around us. They shrieked with laughter, and sometimes fear, as they touched our strange white skin and rubbed the hair on our arms and legs.

What a thrill to eventually hear the testimony of one of the Kukakuka tribal chiefs, "I have lived in deep darkness. I have killed men and eaten them. I have practiced sorcery, fornicated, fought, stolen, and lied. But you have brought a great light to us and I see it! I believe in Jesus Christ!"[210]

Over the years, the Lord opened a wide door of faith to the Menyamya people who are now into their third generation as believers in Christ.

RACKED UP IN RAKAMUNDA

It was Council Karapin, an ex-cannibal war chief who first invited Joe to bring the gospel to the home village of one of his 40 wives. In those days Rakamunda was a 20-hour bone-rattling drive through the highlands (from Lae), followed by a punishing three to five day walk over severe 10,000 foot mountain precipices.

The Rakamunda bush trek is the most grueling I've ever endured. These were 12-14 hour days of tortuous ascents and perilous descents. The ups

---

210   More details of the Kukakuka story is documented in the book *Reckless Abandon*, David Sitton, (Ambassador International, Greenville, SC, 2011), pages 45-60.

were slow, oftentimes vertical, ladder-climbing ascensions, all the while hacking through jungle and warding off biting flies and fire ants. Reaching the summit rewarded us with only a brief reprieve as we walked across the reasonably level plateau before quickly plunging, once again, down the back side bluffs of these seemingly endless alps. The drop-off descents were the most injurious. Once a hiker started a downward sprint, hopping from moss rocks to slippery roots, traversing hidden crevices, and trying to avoid overhanging limbs and jungle vines, all in quick succession down a steep slope, it was difficult to regulate speed and regain firm footing. The gallop sometimes became a dangerous freefall forward and downward, necessitating bumping into trees to break the momentum. Falls were frequent, and broken bones in such remote wilderness could be fatal.

Never underestimate the hazards of traversing river rapids. Mountain streams become furious torrents following a rain. When I noted that Paul had been "in constant danger from rivers,"[211] and he ranked it alongside flogging, shipwrecks, and bandits, I highlighted it in my Bible. Joe did not want any part of angry rivers, and I agree with Paul and Joe on this one! I have nearly died far more often from rivers than thieves. Rivers are not satisfied with your wallet! As Joe said, "You can't negotiate with rivers! They are not impressed with bags of rice [as a gift]."

When it comes to rivers, the choice is either bridge them or swim them, and the conditions of the moment will dictate the decision. In the best of situations you might stumble upon a free swinging, rope-vine bridge that may (or may not) support the weight of your body and gear. These are typically constructed 20 feet or more above the rocks and swirling waters. Although intimidating, if you find a bush bridge, take it with shouts of praise, no questions asked.

A less-attractive bridge option is to locate a tree that someone has already chopped down and laid across the churning chasm. The challenge is to keep your wet, rubber boots firmly atop the slick-as-snot redwood as you inch your way across—and 20 feet above—a thrashing river.

---

211   2 Corinthians 11:26.

If the felled-tree option is the one you are stuck with, there is one other trick-of-the-trade for the experienced bush man. You will have already learned that tumbling off a tree into river rapids is never a good choice, so you jettison self-respect, drop down onto the tree, straddle it with both legs and arms, and scoot on butt and belly across it like a sloth. Joe taught me that impressive maneuver. It does not make for great "Indiana Jones" missionary pictures, but it will keep you out of the morgue. Think survival strategy, not photo op. Remember, even the Apostle Paul was lowered to safety in a basket one time![212]

Finally, failing the bridge options, one might attempt to swim the raging river using ropes and a buddy-system of strong national brothers to drag yourself (or be dragged) across the surging torrent. This is a last resort that brings the morgue back into play.

People groups without Christ usually remain unreached for good geographical reasons. These tribes are impossibly imbedded into nearly inaccessible terrain which necessitates risky, red-alert rescue operations to reach these frontier outposts.[213] Apart from these physical travails, a single bush patrol might include dealing with drunks who break into your hut at night, getting "stoned" by a bunch of kids hurling rocks, coconuts, or corn cobs, and providing refuge for a village councilman whose wife had beaten him with a tree stump.

For a change of pace, I once watched the harrowing experience of one of our carriers get his ailing tooth removed at an isolated jungle "aid-post." He simply laid on the ground while the "expert" knelt over him and twisted, chiseled, and finally broke the tooth off and then dug the rest of it out with a blunt knife (as the patient's legs flailed violently).

Larry Voyles recalls his own Rakamunda expedition with Joe. As he and Tobey Huff prepared a meal of tinned mackerel and rice following a hard day's walk, Joe was taking care of the carriers with their

---

212 Acts 9:25; 2 Corinthians 11:33.

213 Never mind for the moment, the far greater challenge of deep and dark spiritual strangleholds that have suffocated the peoples for centuries.

evening meal.[214] When Joe returned to the campsite "he informed us that one of the female carriers had kindly offered to keep the three of us 'company' that night for two dollars!"[215]

Council Karapin was a short and stout war-chief, hardly the height of my neck. I was teasing him one day, grabbing his shoulders and pretending I was going to throw him off a cliff. He picked me up in a bear hug, draped me over his shoulders and dangled me head first over the edge! He could have disposed of me in an instant. Still flung over his shoulders, he paraded me around in front of the howling villagers. Meanwhile, I reached down and yanked the leaves out of his grass skirt rendering him naked on his backside. He dropped me in the dirt and ran, yelling and laughing into the cover of jungle bushes. That is how you deal with an ex-cannibal war chief from Rakamunda!

As the decade of the 1970s came to a close, Joe had seen to it, through the collaborated efforts of several of us younger missionaries, that a small congregation of believers in Christ had been planted in the remote Rakamunda wilderness. You can see why we called these the Wild West days of PNG mission work!

BUSMAN TRU[216]

Joe truly enjoyed being in the wilderness. He did not relish the physical hardships, but he reveled in being the first one over a ridge or into a new village with the message of Christ—even when he met staunch opposition and violent outbursts (nothing unusual in the 1970s).

---

214 Hard walking patrols sometimes required as many as a dozen carriers, guides, and translators.

215 Why employ female carriers on these rigorous treks? New Guinea women were nearly as strong as the men, often tougher, complained less, and didn't try to renegotiate the carrier price once we were days into the jungle. However, they would sometimes attempt to "supplement" their income with various invitations!

216 Pidgin for "bush man; frontiersman."

When an angry pack of village men confronted us on a bush trek, they made it clear they did not want us on their mountain. Two chiefs wedged themselves into the hut where we were camped and threatened, with much tribal bravado, to kill us later that night. Joe sat on a stool by the fire, listening and drinking his coffee. Then he calmly told the men, "My boys (referring to me and another young missionary) will be asleep in the back room. I'll be asleep right here in the front room." He pointed to his sleeping bag crumpled up next to the entryway of the hut. "When you come back, kill me first because I'm the leader of this team!"

The men slunk out into the night grumbling, and we slept—Joe better than us—without further incident.

In that same region on another occasion, we were similarly endangered. We were exhausted from the long walk of the day. As Joe unpacked our food rations out of a duffel bag he jested, "Well, if they do kill us, at least we won't have to walk back across the mountain!" I think he was only half-joking. This sort of thing happened frequently on the gospel trail with Joe. He really did not care if he lived or died; he only wanted to be faithful in carrying the gospel into new places. This was the sole ambition of his life.

Many admired Joe, but few were able to walk with him for very long. I do not mean on a particular day, but in his dogged perseverance over the course of decades. I could out-hike Joe (my 20 years versus his 50), but only barely. In my youthful impatience I charged way ahead of him, but he did not care. He laughed at us "young bucks who tore up the trails during the day." But he was proud of the fact and let it be known that "we always sleep in the same hut every night!" Some of us were fast, but he was steady. Joe often reminded us of the wisdom gleaned from Rick Niland's experience as a patrol officer, "Take it easy, boys. In big mountains, walk fifteen minutes and rest for five. In the really big ones, walk five and rest fifteen, if you must. Pace yourself and you can walk all the way to the moon!"

READY, AIM, FIRE: THE 25-YEAR STRATEGIC PLAN

Run in such a way as to get the prize . . . Not like a man running aimlessly . . . Not like a boxer beating the air; I do this for the sake of the gospel to win as many as possible.

1 Corinthians 9:24-26

"Plan the Work; Work the Plan."

Joe Cannon

Joe Cannon loved maps, statistics, and strategy meetings, but he was not an armchair general. First and finally, Joe was a church planting practitioner. Between 1971 and 1975 more than 20 congregations were established, primarily in the coastal areas of Morobe and the Eastern

Joe loved maps!

Highlands. The congregation in Lae swelled towards 300 believers and the School of Life buzzed with the excitement of its first year students. Joe was elated by the speedy spread of the gospel but envisaged even more widespread headway.

Joe's constant Matthew 9:38 prayer for "harvest laborers" resulted in a sudden and robust surge of missionary manpower. The influx of workforces, together with the receptivity of the local people, compelled him to even more enthused prayer and unrestrained tactical brainstorming. Joe studied Scripture, schemed over PNG maps, and hurriedly penciled rapid-fire, country-sized dreams into his prayer journals. His escalating missiological convictions were bolstered through a New Testament word study from First and Second Corinthians. He made particular note of the words "aim" and "strategy": "Aim," *adeilos* in Greek, is defined as a "definite, certain plan of action."[217] The word "strategy" (*strateigia*) is translated as "warfare" or "weapons" and used at least 59 times in the New Testament.[218]

Joe concluded that an aimless no-win missionary strategy is unscriptural. Following the Apostle Paul's mission in the Book of Acts, Joe mused, "Paul didn't merely roam around the Roman Empire in a haphazard fashion. He had plans for where he went and for what he would do when he got there."[219] Joe was emboldened when he realized how the Lord frequently exercised his divine prerogative to alter Paul's travel plans,[220] but Paul still made plans, followed hard after them, and trusted that the Lord would get him where He wanted him in the harvest. Joe carefully held the tension tight between the necessities of following the Holy Spirit spontaneously and the imperative of devising tactical plans for evangelistic advancement. For Joe, there was no contradiction between prayer for direction and faith evidenced by immediate, aggressive action.

In all of this excitement the seed of a vision rattled around within Joe's heart and head. However, it was far from full-blown. What he did have was a biblical rationale for the necessity of a definite strategy and a fast-growing team of young (and old) missionaries who were on board and eager to help him get it done.

Early in 1978, Joe organized a three-day retreat for the entire missionary team: men, women, children, dogs, and pigs (as Joe joked). More than 50 of us gathered for a "prayer, brain-storming, and strategic planning" meeting in the small town of Kainantu. Art Ford served as chairman for the meetings. Passionate prayer for PNG, unrestrained (and humorous) brainstorming, and animated give-and-take debates more than

---

217 A Greek-English Lexicon to the New Testament, William Greenfield (published prior to 1923). Revised by T.S. Green (1976). This book was one of Joe's study resources.

218 The New Englishman's Greek Concordance, (1972), page 700. William Carey Library, Pasadena, CA.

219 Joe Cannon. Undated sermon notes.

220 Acts 16:6-10, for example.

balanced out the bogged-down times of parsing laborious details and deliberations. The blueprint for a 25-Year Strategic Plan for the evangelization of PNG was the exhilarating result of the gathering.

The focus of the plan was to create a gospel presence throughout the key strategic cities of PNG with the goal of saturating the remote village areas in every direction out of those towns. Five key strategic cities were identified as the initial targets for missionary activity with 16 additional rural towns as second-tier strategic sites.

Mapping a 25-Year Strategic Plan

5 KEY STRATEGIC CENTERS	16 STRATEGIC CENTERS
Lae	Wau, Popondetta, Wewak, and Orouba
Goroka	Madang and Kainantu
Port Moresby	Kerema, Daru, and Alotau
Mt. Hagen	Kundiawa, Mendi, Wabag, and Tari
Rabaul	Lorengau, Kavieng, and Arawa

Each Key Strategic Center required five missionary units (married and/or single) focusing on:

- Local Church Development
- Bible Training School
- Outreach to Un-evangelized Areas
- Medical (benevolence) Ministries
- Business Manager / Secretary

The estimated necessary team for all five key strategic centers = 25 missionary units.

Each of the Strategic Centers required two missionary units focusing on:
- In-reach (local church development)
- Out-reach (un-evangelized areas)

The estimated necessary team for the 16 strategic centers = 32 missionary units.

Total number of personnel necessary for the 21 key and strategic centers = 57 missionary units.

This strategic plan provided for a significant gospel presence in each of the 21 PNG provinces.[221]

Over the next 13 years[222] four of the 5 Key Strategic Centers and seven of the 21 Strategic Centers were at least partially manned and operational. This flurry of gospel advance resulted in at least 200 congregations scattered throughout the 23 provinces of PNG, including three Bible schools.

No doubt, thousands of Papua New Guineans have been swept into the kingdom of Christ through these gospel efforts. Every soul saved is a testimony to the grace of God. Ever the statistician, Joe was quick to record numbers, both the good and not-so-good ones. Either way, he was insistent on telling the truth of the story. I admire the honesty in his evaluations and reports of the successes and setbacks in the PNG work. One example is a brutally honest handwritten list of highlands congregations that, for various reasons, were no longer meeting.[1]

---

221 There were 21 provinces in PNG in 1978. There are presently 23 provinces as the Hela and Jiwaka provinces were sub-divided out of the Southern Highlands and the Western Highlands provinces respectively in 2012.

222 Brief summaries of work in the Key Strategic Centers and Strategic Centers are overviewed in the PNG Team booklet entitled "Walking in Yesterday (1979)," last known revision (1985).

PNG NATIONAL MISSIONARIES[II]

The number of Papua New Guineans who were converted to Christ and became faithful co-workers alongside expatriate missionaries is impossible to accurately track. God only knows the work for Christ that was accomplished through their sacrifices. But the Lord knows, and He knows where to find them for their day of reward.

Among this group were former thieves, murderers, prostitutes, beggars, young teens and old codgers, coastal peoples and highlanders, stone-aged and college-educated. All of these were caught in the gracious net of the gospel and many of them courageously became the "tip of the gospel spear" which carried salvation to many of their own traditional tribal enemies. Joe sometimes referred to these national missionaries as a herd of "Menakamp,"[223] and the people hollered proudly at his accolade. The world needs many more of these stout-hearted warriors for Jesus.

One of these is Miamel Golabe, one of five SOL students who accompanied me on a hard-hiking gospel patrol to Engati (one of the clans of the Menyamya people).[224] The last time I was with him, he flashed his handsome smile and said with a boisterous laugh, "You asked me to go with you to Menyamya in 1981, and I've been working with them ever since!" Miamel served alongside missionaries such as Nancy Merritt, Andrew Jackson, Woody Square, and others unknown to me, establishing several congregations scattered around the Menyamya Mountains, and at least one more located in the "Tent City" suburb of Lae. I mention Miamel here because he is still serving as a national brother cut from the same tough and persevering missionary cloth as Joe Cannon.

Neme Mile (pronounced *Me-Lay*), another dear brother and late-1970s student in the SOL, deserves honorable mention as well. Neme was a

---

223 "Menakamp" = "Wild pigs" in one of the highland languages. Larry Voyles. Reminisces (2011).

224 The difficulties (two days in a canoe and a five-day walk), near loss of life, and eventual helicopter rescue are documented in the book, *In The Hearts of Wild Men*, Ernest Herndon, (Grace and Truth Books, Sand Springs, OK, 1986).

New Guinea highlander who was killed in a river accident while serving Christ in the tough Menyamya Mountains during the late 1980s.

Papua New Guinean missionaries with the Churches of Christ have served in 17 of the 23 PNG provinces and Vanuatu in the New Hebrides, the Solomon Islands, and (Papua) Indonesia.

EXPATRIATE MISSIONARIES[III]

It is likewise impossible to precisely detail all of the good work done by so many expatriate missionaries. These also have followed in Joe and RB's footsteps and sacrificed much to extend the gospel into harsh environments. Not all of these came out of the mission unscathed. Some have buried children on foreign soil, as Joe and RB did with Ivy Rose in Okinawa. Rex and Brenda Morgan had a baby daughter die of a fast-acting viral infection in PNG. Fred and Sandra Burroughs also grieved the death of their son in the states while they were still in PNG. No doubt, others have suffered similarly but are unknown to me.

Dale Templeton is a few inches shorter than he used to be following a horrific head-on car crash on the Highlands highway. Dale severely broke both legs and was very nearly killed. Sadly one person in the other vehicle was killed.

Frequently dengue,[225] malarial fevers, and the ravages of tropical ulcers and parasitic amoebas plagued the missionaries. Ruth Coles suffered significant hearing loss due to long-term use of anti-malarial medicines. David Lock's missionary career was suddenly ended by severe amoebic dysentery. I nearly died from two separate bouts of Black Water[226] Fever. Countless incidents of dehydration and mental, physical, and emotional exhaustion were not uncommon for many of us.

---

225 Joe called it "broke-bone" fever.

226 Black Water Fever is an uncommon, yet dangerous, form of malaria. Symptoms include rapid pulse, high fever and chills, extreme prostration, anemia, and black urine. It seldom appears until one has had at least four attacks of malaria and has been in an endemic area for six months.

Our national brothers and sisters have borne with us an equal share of the inherent hardship required to advance Jesus' name in PNG. For them, the fear of traveling into regions where traditional enemies resided was enormous. Their lives were often endangered in ways we never even realized. They served us well when they selflessly volunteered to carry the heaviest bags of Bibles, food, clothing, and bedding. Many times our national brothers and sisters nursed us back to health in remote mountain outposts and jungles so that gospel patrols were possible.

Premature deaths, multiple illnesses, accidents, broken bones, and destroyed livers, kidneys, knees, and backs are all part of the ground-zero casualties that hindered—but did not stop—a great gospel light from being shone into the darkness of New Guinea. The survivors walk with a limp but, I daresay, with few regrets.

Still others have been crippled by the scars of sin, some have agonized through depression and divorce, and a few have fallen away from the Lord altogether. But still the gospel marches on.

My best effort[227] to identify the missionaries who served in PNG (two years minimum) totaled at least 84 missionary units (families). These units represent 129 adult individuals and hundreds of children from at least seven countries (USA, Canada, Australia, Japan, Holland, Scotland, and Ireland).

The Lord graciously responded to Joe's prayers for laborers, so much so that some in North America complained about the seeming inequity of so much missionary firepower in PNG, compared to other countries. Joe's response was characteristically Cannon-esque: "If they want more workers they should do what I did. Get to work asking the Lord of the Harvest for them!"

Joe wasn't unconcerned about the shortage of workers on other fields, but he was realistic about the immensity of the gospel challenge in PNG. He confronted the criticism:[228]

---

227   My apologies in advance for any unintended omissions in this missionary list. Be encouraged! The Lord knows who you are and the sacrifices you have made for the gospel in PNG.

228   Joe Cannon missionary report (adapted for brevity), February 2, 1978.

"But Joe, you're asking for too many workers." My answer to this is that if we continue to function in mission as we have in the past, we will never evangelize the world.

There are men and women sufficient for the task, and money too. But to this point, we have not had the heart for it. We have been playing around with missionary work in a number of countries, but with no real strategy to take those countries for Christ. I tell you, brethren, we are so used to doing a half-baked, piddling job in countries around the world that we don't know what it's like to really do a job on a country for Christ!

I admit that I am sometimes awfully tired of driving these roads, climbing these mountains and sitting on the dirt floors on a stack of wood in smoke-filled bush huts preaching for hours after an exhausting day. I know we lean on you for all kinds of help, but do not be weary. We are gospel partners. Your sacrifice on that side is complimented by what we do on this side. We determine to pray for and use the manpower and money necessary to accomplish this gospel purpose, and we make no excuses and feel no hesitancy in seeking the men and money for this task. If this stirs up frustrations or jealousies among others working in other lands, all I can say is, "Go thou and do likewise." Let's get the gospel to every creature in our generation and stop making excuses for not doing it.

PART 5: MISSION/1000 (1984-1997)

Mission/1000 was born in the bosom of prayer.

Larry McKenzie

LARRY AND LOIS VOYLES INITIATED a difficult church planting effort into the New Guinea highlands in 1980, and Joe and RB soon followed to assist in developing Mt. Hagen as one of our strategic field bases. Always the Pied Piper, Joe led a small band of missionaries into the interior. Mt. Hagen quickly became a beehive of mission activity.

Ray and Elizabeth Lock, Paul and Linda McAnally, and Tommi and I were among the repositioned workforce[229] from Lae. The gospel was on the rapid upswing as a local congregation was reinforced, first contacts for the gospel were forged in the most remote mountain outposts, and the Mt. Hagen Bible School was organized with a handful of rowdy young believers.

ON-THE-GO TRAINING

With a solid strategy enacted and a burgeoning influx of newly arrived missionaries beginning to occupy the strategic centers, Joe's pioneer soul was again alerted and drawn to attention. As early as 1979, he had

---

229 An essential piece of the 25-Year Strategic Plan was for veteran missionaries to train rookie recruits.

envisioned a new missionary training program and brainstormed the idea for several years with his old friend Larry McKenzie.

In January 1983, Joe and Larry approached the elders at the Highland Church of Christ in Memphis, Tennessee, with the vision of *Mission 1000*. When asked to describe the M/1000 vision, Joe said, "To surface, train and field 1,000 new missionaries for the ends of the earth!" Classic, uncompromising Joe!

GOING WITH THE GOSPEL AND GETTING OTHERS TO GO WITH THE GOSPEL WAS JOE'S *GREAT COMMISSION* IN LIFE.

M/1000 aimed to provide basic training courses designed to quickly mobilize many for cross-cultural ministry. The proposed schedule allowed Joe and RB to continue going with the gospel themselves during large chunks of each calendar year. The M/1000 strategy was shaped in large part by three missionaries who unknowingly impressed on Joe an angle to missionary partnership that could be incredibly advantageous to the speedier spread of the gospel.

Bob Herndon was an old friend from Joe's and RB's days in Okinawa. When Bob retired from a successful career in civil service, Joe challenged him for PNG. Bob's arrival coincided perfectly with the rapid increase of new missionaries who needed long-term visas and work permits. Wise in the ways of government bureaucracy, Bob skillfully traversed multiple layers of administrative red tape and, over four years of self-supporting ministry, acquired more than 90 visas for the incoming workforce.

The scarcity of affordable housing options was worsened by the fast-growing missionary team. Thankfully, the shortfall was greatly relieved when the Lord landed Mel and Donna Bowman in Lae. Mel was an Aggie[230] architect and building contractor from central Texas. Virtually upon arrival, Joe corralled Mel to work alongside him to develop plans for a Missionary Center to be constructed on the edge of the Boundary Road property. The project encountered numerous work stoppages but, with Mel's architec-

---

230 Nickname for a student or former student of Texas A & M University.

tural abilities, Joe's fundraising, and the grunt labor of many, the task was accomplished.[231] Mel and Donna later relocated to Mt. Hagen to construct missionary houses, a modest church building, and several small structures that served the needs of the Mt. Hagen Bible School.

Florence Gelley, an elderly widow from Canada, meekly approached Joe after one of his meetings in Toronto. "Is there anything an old woman like me can offer to the spread of the gospel in PNG?" Joe retorted, "Ask the Lord of the harvest, He'll tell you!" Florence prayed, Jesus said "Yes," and she courageously accepted the challenge to raise her own support. She devoted five of her last years on earth to the Lae team. She served as an encourager, on-site prayer warrior, and confidant to single missionaries. Florence blessed PNG women by teaching them to sew and being a loving "grandma" to both national and missionary children alike. She was small in stature, but never lacked the guts, gusto, and joyful faith to get her hands dirty in the work of loving people to Christ.

JOE ONCE SAID TO FLORENCE IN NEW GUINEA, "DON'T BE AFRAID. YOU'RE AS CLOSE TO HEAVEN IN PNG AS YOU WERE IN CANADA!"

Any missionary team would be strengthened by a woman like Florence Gelley. She finally returned to Canada as an 80 plus-year-old woman whom had refused to waste her final years.

Joe eagerly identified meaningful places of service for these "helpers" of missionaries who he considered so essential to the success of the mission. They brought proficiency in skills that missionaries could not or did not have time or energy to accomplish. At the same time, he recognized that these *missionaries* also would benefit from the right kind of basic training in theology and missiology which would substantially maximize their field effectiveness.

Joe foresaw M/1000 as a place to quickly prepare and propel believers of any age, gender, or skill set into cross-cultural service alongside

---

231 The Mission Center consisted of eight small bedrooms, four on each side of a common kitchen, men/women shower rooms, and a large meeting room.

M/1000, 1st graduating class (1984)

veteran missionaries. Joe coined[232] this "Para-Missionary" training. A "para-missionary" is an "assistant" in the work of mission. "Para" from the Greek is translated as "with" or "alongside." Just as a "paramedic" is one who gives assistance to medical workers, so the para-missionary helps missionaries in vital supportive roles. Para-missionaries actively used their practical skills as carpenters, electricians, administrators, attorneys, nurses, teachers, mechanics, printers, pilots, secretaries, as well as Bible teachers—all for the purpose of *helping* to spread the gospel of Christ worldwide.

When the Highland Church leadership heard the M/1000 proposal in 1983, they promptly determined that the ministry should be implemented as quickly as possible. Energized by the swift decision of the elders, Joe and Rosa Belle made their move to Memphis shortly after Christmas to establish the training center. The inaugural class of M/1000 began on September 10, 1984, with 12 trainees. A year later, at the beginning of the third session of M/1000, Joe wrote:[233]

> By God's good grace, M/1000 is off the ground. We're not flying high yet, but we are moving along. Including our present students, we have trained 42, which leaves us 958 to go! We expect most of the 42 will be "fielded" by the end of this year in 13 countries. We are encouraged by the results the Lord has given us.

---

232 Joe used the phrase "para-missionary" as early as 1980.

233 Mission/1000 Newsletter (1985), Vol. 1 No. 2.

Joe's summation following the completion of the sixth session:[234]

> Ten more are off to serve the Lord in the mission fields of the world.
> The total number trained is 70. Half of them are in the mission.

ON-THE-GO ENCOURAGEMENT

INDONESIA (1990-1996)

During the M/1000 summer breaks, Joe and RB retraced their missionary steps to encourage their brethren in Japan, Okinawa and PNG.

Cold water highlands baptism

But Joe was also interested in breaking some new ground of his own. Squeezed in between the fifth and sixth sessions of M/1000 in 1987, Joe and Rosa Belle bolted for the South Pacific to visit the work in Papua New Guinea and to explore new ministry possibilities with their old friend Duane Morgan in Irian Jaya, Indonesia.[235]

Knowing that Tommi and I focused our church planting efforts from Wewak, on the north coast of PNG, Joe informed me that their flight would refuel and lay over for a while in our town. This was classic Cannon modus operandi. Joe and RB highly valued missionaries and rarely missed an opportunity to seek out and encourage co-workers from the past wherever they might be in the world. They expended great effort and expense to visit former colleagues, national brethren, and congregations on their fast and furious on-the-go encouragement journeys.

---

234 Mission/1000 Report, November 23, 1987.

235 Duane Morgan e-mail, July 5, 2014.

In 1987 Joe and RB made their first foray into Irian Jaya[236], a province of Indonesia located on the western side of the island of New Guinea. When Duane returned to Irian Jaya in 1990, they visited several times over the next six years, primarily teaching alongside Duane in the Bible school he established in Serui on month-long teaching stints. This fruitful collaboration continued into the mid-1990s when the school acquired permanent facilities at Urei Faisei.

Joe reported that eight congregations were established in Irian Jaya by 1992.[237] In a Cannon newsletter later that year, Duane described the ministry of encouragement that Joe and RB brought on these missionary jaunts:[238]

> Joe and Rosa Belle are missionaries of 45 years' experience. They have seen about every condition imaginable on land and sea. The next session of M/1000 begins on September 1st, and they've already been away from Memphis for 3 months on an arduous missionary journey to Japan, PNG, and Irian Jaya.
>
> Their visits are a highlight of our year. Joe and RB are perpetually young and invariably optimistic. I can assure you that these are real working trips, not leisurely excursions . . . Joe taught at the school and gave us priceless encouragement . . . Receive them with respect and honor . . . They have risked their lives for the sake of the gospel and they have refreshed our spirits.

CHURCH OF CHRIST HISTORY IN RUSSIA

[Author's Note: This section on Belarus and a later one on

---

236 Now renamed Papua, Indonesia.

237 Winter Report from the Cannons, February, 1992.

238 Cannon Report (undated). Duane references Joe's 45 years of mission experience, which would make it 1992.

Ukraine—both republics of the former Soviet Union—will be en-
hanced and better understood by this brief historical perspective.]

The Churches of Christ have loose roots twisting deep into Russian history at least as far back as 1874.[239] A wealthy landowner, Vasily Pashkov, led a spiritual revival among the Russian nobility and invested considerable finances to circulate Bibles and teaching materials to bring "dissenters" against the Orthodox Church into a unified fellowship. He was moderately successful but was finally exiled in 1884.

Ivan Prokhanov, a Pashkov disciple, started an engineering career in St. Petersburg in 1888. Ivan was a man of great energy and a passion for "biblical Christianity." He led the "evangelical Christians" for 40 years until his departure from Russia in 1928. The assumed reason he left Russia was the start of the Stalinist era with its firm determination to stamp out Christianity from the region. However, by then, a substantial movement, numbering several million "Bible-only"[240] believers, was scattered across the vast land of Russia. The historical thread was largely broken by Russian intolerance for Christianity in 1928, but not completely.

Wesley Jones and Geoff Ellis scoured the St. Petersburg libraries during a week of concentrated research in 1991. They discovered partial writings of Prokhanov and his publication "The Christian" preserved in the Saltykov-Shchedrin State Public Library.[241] The following two weeks were to be spent in Moscow, but an unexpected coup[242] attempt abruptly ended the

---

239 Wesley Jones and Geoff Ellis collaborated in research seeking confirmation of a Russian restoration-like movement during 1870-1930. Historical data taken from "Report on 3rd Journey to Russia" (April, 1993) Geoff Ellis.

240 Also called "The Christians," "Evangelical Christians," "The Bible-only Church" or the "Pashkovite Movement."

241 The Museum of Religion and Atheism in the grand Kazan Cathedral houses these literary archives and artifacts.

242 This was the failed coup of August 19-21, 1991. President Mikhail Gorbachev was not immediately overthrown but eventually lost out to Boris Yeltsin.

research expedition.[243] When they returned the following year, all traces of Pashkov's influence had been removed from the Moscow library archives.[244]

BELARUS (1994-1997)

Freddie Galos and Sasha Yefimenko, two young Russian men eager to learn about North American cultural practices, embarked upon a research outing of their own.[245] They traveled the southern United States, lodging with American families along the way.

Faye Moore, from Alabama, volunteered to be a host family for the young men. Before they arrived, she prayed that her family would be a good Christian witness to them. The Moore family opened their home and hearts to Freddie and Sasha, so much so that Freddie told his mother Natasha, back in Minsk, that he had "fallen in love" with the whole family. Natasha spoke English well enough that she replied with wholehearted gratitude for Faye's kindness and thanked her profusely for sending her the first Bible that she had ever seen. This, of course, deepened the friendship and opened the way for Faye to share the gospel more directly.

Unaware of any believers in Belarus, but through a series of providential contacts, Faye learned of a missionary in Bulgaria, whose name was Russ Burcham. Russ and his wife visited Natasha and her husband Nicholi in Belarus and stayed for three weeks. Nicholi and Natasha, along with Lydia Loginova, believed in Christ and were baptized in September, 1991. By that time, Sasha had returned from his stateside trip. He believed the gospel, too, and a small church of four people began in their home.

---

243 Wesley and Geoff made two more research ventures into Russia resulting in the book, *The Other Revolution: Russian Evangelical Awakenings* (1996). Geoffrey Ellis and Wesley Jones. ACU Press, Abilene, Texas.

244 The Moscow library was the central library in the U.S.S.R.

245 Edited for brevity from, *The Beginnings of the Church in Minsk*, Belarus (1991), author unknown.

Converging with these relational developments between Alabama and Belarus was a third providential occurrence in Texas. Missionary Allen Borden visited the Walnut Street Church of Christ in Texarkana and spoke about his desire to "adopt" a city in the Soviet Union using the means of friendship to share the gospel. Brothers A.D. Smith and Ron Boatwright caught his enthusiasm and agreed to an exploratory trip to investigate the possibilities.

As the old Soviet Union was dissolving in 1991 (following the coup attempt), A.D. Smith led a group from Texarkana with the express purpose of choosing a city in Russia to adopt for friendship. At the same time, Russ Burcham contacted Allen Borden[246] in the Soviet Union with the specific request for someone to come and teach the new Christian family in Belarus. The Texarkana team arrived in Kiev (Ukraine) and learned about the previously unknown need for fellowship and teaching in Belarus. Recognizing this as a possible answer to their own prayer for guidance, A.D. and five others boarded an overnight train to the city of Minsk. The group stayed with Nicholi and Natasha with the result that a strong friendship was forged and five more believed the gospel during the week-long visit.

A.D. returned to Texarkana with the recommendation that Minsk should become their city for adoption, and the congregation joyfully approved. Several teams from Walnut Street followed in quick succession, encouraging new believers and visiting schools, hospitals, orphanages and individual homes, and sharing the love and gospel of Christ. Follow-up trips focused upon basic Bible teaching and organizing the Christ-followers into a local congregation that had quickly grown to more than 60 believers.

INTO THIS FLURRY OF PROVIDENTIAL ADVANCEMENT OF THE GOSPEL

(IN THE FORMER SOVIET UNION) STRODE JOE AND RB!

They leapt into the Belarus opportunity with both feet, Bibles, and suitcases. This was a dream come true for Joe. His journals from the

---

246 Tragically, Allen Borden was killed in an automobile accident north of Dallas, TX, the following year (1992). A.D. Smith e-mail, July 29, 2014.

1980s include direct prayers for the dissolution of Russia "for the good of the gospel" and for the doors of Russia to "blow wide open" for Christ!

Shortly after arrival in Belarus while sitting on the fifth floor balcony of the Orbita Hotel in Minsk, Joe jubilantly scribbled:[247]

> How wonderful to be greeted by smiling, loving Christians! All praise to the glorious God of heaven and earth who opened up for himself this door of opportunity,[248] and praise to the authority of His Son who "dashed to pieces"[249] the Soviet Empire and "rules the nations with an iron scepter."[250]

Armed with his usual historical perspective about the places he labored, Joe continued:

> The new republic of Belarus! But not so new. They have kept their identity through the centuries although run over by many invasions – the Iranians, Macedonians, Celts, Germans-Goths, Sarmiatians, Huns, Bulgers, Avars, Slavs, Tartars . . . But preceding all of this from 700 B.C. on, the Greeks established a strong presence followed by the Romans. The Greek name for the wild nomadic inhabitants of Russia was "Scythians."[251]

> Western-oriented Europeans hardly appreciate how the early gospel spread into all the world, along the Roman highways, up into Romania and the influence of three Macedonian churches (Philippi, Thessalonica, Berea) . . . All on the Roman road, all with ancient ties with the Scythians – Russians!

---

247 Newsletter "From Joe and Rosa Belle about Minsk, Belarussia" (1994).

248 Acts 14:27; 2 Corinthians 2:12.

249 Psalm 2:9.

250 Revelation 12:5.

251 Colossians 3:10-11.

It is wonderful today to have a small part in the renewal of Christianity into the land of the Scythians!

BELARUS BIBLE COLLEGE

Belarus Bible College was not really a college. The brethren in Minsk called it a "college" because of the value they put on the teaching of Scripture, and in characteristic Cannon-esque fashion, it was intense. Joe and two other men taught for 175 hours, meeting seven hours a day, five days a week, for five weeks. The theme was: The Big Ideas of the New Testament Books. Five translators were worn out as 40 major subjects were taught from the Gospels, Acts, the Epistles, and Revelation. Then, because of frigid temperatures, new believers were baptized (with much difficulty) in Joe and RB's small hotel bathtub as the Lord saved them.

A similar schedule was followed for five weeks a year for four years.[252] At the conclusion of one such teaching marathon, Joe remarked:[253]

> We had a high attendance of 75 in our classes. The church in Minsk is maturing nicely and carrying on their work faithfully. Six men have been chosen for more specific leadership training.
>
> We don't know how long the Lord will allow us the privilege of serving Him, but we intend to keep at it as long as we have breath.

Ever the pioneers, after a month of full-time teaching, Joe and RB would sometimes go into the southernmost parts of Russia to preach the gospel. I do not know the details of how or what they

---

252 This small start resulted in a preaching school, the "Higher Private Humanitarian College" (avoiding overtly Christian terminology to satisfy Belarusian requirements). The school is almost completely self-supporting and self-taught by local brothers. Graduates now serve other cities throughout Belarus. A.D. Smith e-mail (July 29, 2014). See also the 21st Century Global Missions website (www.21stcgm.com).

253 Joe Cannon Newsletter, January, 1995.

did, I only know that Joe mentioned these excursions in his journals. Through his own work and that of others, at least 80 congregations[254] were started in various places throughout some of the far-reaching regions of the former Soviet Union. They did all of this at age 68 (Joe) and 72 (RB).

LIFE EVENTS

Joe Cannon's Books (1991-1993): Mission 1000 semesters were scheduled throughout the spring and fall months. Sandwiched between sessions, Joe and RB crisscrossed the globe on annual mission trips through the summer and wintered in Canada. During three consecutive Canadian winters, Joe authored three books[255] to coincide with his upcoming M/1000 classes.

Joe and RB's Involvement with Social and Sin Issues (1987-1996): Joe and RB were not cultural bystanders in the Memphis community. They joined in "Walk for the Homeless" rallies that included a program to help the homeless get from the streets into housing and jobs; they were involved in anti-abortion demonstrations; and they cared for those ensnared by substance addictions. Joe was particularly distressed by the ravages of pornography upon society. In numerous entries in his prayer journals, he specifically interceded against *Hustler Magazine* and 7-11 convenience stores that openly marketed pornography at checkout counters. He vigorously prayed "against the demonic powers behind the Playboy channel."[256] Even as Joe boldly prayed for the dissolution of Russia for the swifter advance of the gospel, he also asked the Lord to "overthrow and defeat the demons" of pornography, abortion, poverty, and drug addiction for the glory of God . . . And he rejoiced that at least

---

254 Many were small house churches.

255 *The Heart of the Missionary* (self-published, 1994); *Go for the Globe* (self-published, 1994); and *God's Own Love* (unpublished, 1990 or 1993).

256 Example: on Jan. 22, 1986 he asked the Lord "to cast out the demons of porn and abortion." On April 22, 1986, he praised God for answered prayer when he read somewhere that "porn sales had dropped at 7-11!"

four people had come to Christ through those efforts.

Joe Cannon's Health Issues (1989-1994): Joe began to have heart concerns in 1989, but moseyed along into the new decade until he was diagnosed with aortic stenosis, diabetes, and skin cancer. Surgery in 1994 corrected the heart and skin cancer concerns, diabetes was controlled by diet and exercise, and his "bad" back was simply tolerated.

Death of a Rideau Rat (1995): Murray Hammond[257] was one of Joe's closest friends, dating back

50 Years of Marriage and Mission

to their teenaged years as the "Rideau Rats" on the streets of Toronto. Murray came to faith in Christ about the same time as Joe and became a preacher of the gospel for many years, but he also suffered with poor health most of his life. When Joe learned that his old friend was near death, he called to encourage him:

> "Hey Murray, what's this I hear about you getting ready to go to heaven? You dirty rat, I'm the Skipper of the Rideau Rats and I should go to Heaven before you!"

> Murray bantered back, "That's too bad for you, Joe; eat your heart out!"

> Vintage Joe. They had a good laugh, said their goodbyes, and Joe wrote, "Well, Murray went on and I'm still here. But I look forward to the day when I'll join him with the Lord we loved so much and about whom we both have preached so much."

---

257 Murray Hammond was born on May 30, 1929, and died April 13, 1995 (age 66).

Joe's Very Public Parking Ticket: Joe and Rosa Belle were awarded the Distinguished Alumnus Award at Harding College in 1997. When university president Dr. David Burke introduced him, Joe sauntered across the stage and greeted his outstretched hand with a wadded up parking ticket that the campus police had just awarded him. Dr. Burke was a bit embarrassed when Joe asked if he "could do something about the ticket" in front of more than 2,000 people! Some laughed at the humor, others thought it awkward. But this was Joe's way to make light of his own importance and deflect praise away from himself. He followed up the joke with a brief, but thoughtful acceptance of the award and gave praise to God for the privilege he and RB had to serve Christ in Japan, Okinawa, and PNG.

50 YEARS OF MARRIAGE AND MISSION

By the conclusion of the 18th M/1000 session, Joe and RB were obviously slowing down.[258]

> This year everything turns 50 . . . 50 years gloriously married and 50 years of involvement in missionary work. I am now 70 and RB is 74 and we will never *voluntarily* [author emphasis] retire. The only one who can retire us is our wonderful Chief Missionary in Heaven. He took us on and He is the only one who can take us off!

However, Joe knew a secret that he was not yet willing to reveal. Obvious to Joe and others close to her was that Rosa Belle had begun to experience significant memory loss. Without disclosing her condition, but in this same letter, Joe updated their ministry activities:[259]

> I taught five hours a day for a month in Canada,[260] preached a gospel meeting in Battle Axe, Texas, and taught two prayer seminars

---

258 Missionary newsletter, February 21, 1997.

259 Ibid.

260 Great Lakes Bible College, Waterloo, Ontario, an extension of Great Lakes Christian College, Beamsville, Ontario.

in Waterloo, Ontario, and Williamsport, PA. I have preached and taught 121 times. I say this only to let you know that RB and I are in good health. How long we can continue only God knows, but we have no interest in stopping because of age!

Joe prayed in a December 11, 1990 journal entry:

Courage for the home stretch and victories over ageing for your glory (December 11, 1990).

Joe and RB had a fatiguing policy of back-tracking their missionary steps through (at least) Japan, Okinawa, and PNG every year.[261] In an April 29, 1996 letter to supporters, Joe vowed:

We will never desert our overseas children and grandchildren in the gospel and the churches we have begun, as long as we are able to make these missionary journeys. When it becomes impossible for us to travel we will still encourage the harvest fields with our faith and prayers.

No wonder Joe was physically and emotionally exhausted. However, this is the hectic itinerary Joe maintained for most of his life. Once, in a phone conversation with Cliff Cobb (an elder at Stamford, Texas), Joe said, "You know, Cliff, our luggage seems to get heavier every year" (a not so veiled reference to his increasing weariness). Cliff wisely countered, "If you want to know what's wrong with you, Joe, look at your calendar!" Joe chuckled and said, "Thanks, Cliff, I think I'll go take a nap!" But he never slowed down.

With sadness and reluctant awareness, he added to the newsletter:[262]

At the present time we are preparing for the spring session (19th) of M/1000, but it looks like we do not have the required

261 Some years they added Indonesia or Belarus to their travel plans.

262 Ibid.

number to justify the effort. We have the rule of at least five in order to have a go, which we have done for 13 years.

There are special events later in this anniversary year. One is a general meeting of Churches of Christ on April 29th, to celebrate 50 post-war years of the church in Ibaraki (Joe was a guest speaker) . . . Next, our children and grandchildren are preparing an anniversary celebration for us . . . After this we will be, Lord willing, traveling to Irian Jaya, Indonesia and PNG to teach and encourage the brethren there. Five of our M/1000 students are in PNG and we want to see how they are doing.

Keep praying for us and especially for our M/1000 graduates who are serving Christ all over the world.

Joe and RB's final worldwide mission year together was 1996. He preached at the 50th anniversary celebration of their ministry in Japan, and later that year they visited Indonesia and Papua New Guinea for the final time. A family reunion wedged between these two arduous overseas treks proved to be the last time the entire Cannon clan was all together in one location, while Joe and RB were still living.

UNWELCOME TRANSITIONS

Cannon Family Reunion (June 1997): The Cannon children organized a relaxed family get-together at the Victory Valley Encampment, near Memphis. Robin Cannon remembers the gathering as comfortable but with a formal tone, as everyone understood in advance the announcement that would be confirmed. Rosa Belle was suffering from progressive memory loss and needed increasing care, and Joe was determined to be the one who would give it to her. It was no longer possible for their high-octane, *Go for the Globe* lives to be sustained at the usual breakneck pace.

M/1000: Short-term goals for M/1000 for the remainder of 1997 became two-fold:

- Determine if M/1000 had any additional future with the Highland Church

- If so, find a director to replace Joe Cannon

When no replacement was found, M/1000 ceased to exist and Joe and RB prepared to return to Okinawa to work with Robin and Cyndi. Joe notified his supporting churches and friends:[263]

> This letter is to inform you concerning important changes. The first is the impending retirement of Rosa Belle and me. We are now in our 70's and it has been 13 years since the Lord blessed us with the inauguration of M/1000. We feel that it is time for others to carry it on. It has not yet reached 1,000, having only trained 220. But we believe firmly that the Lord will give us one thousand in his own good time and good way.
>
> Therefore, we want to return to Okinawa and work again as full time missionaries. *[Author's Note: Didn't he just announce "retirement" in the previous paragraph?]* We want to assist Robin and Cyndi in their work with a new congregation in Chibana. We have a five-year plan in which to do this, along with encouraging church plantings and being of service to the churches on the main islands of Japan.

As the 19th and final class of M/1000 came to an end, Joe and RB packed up for a final missionary stint in Okinawa. This was Joe's concept of *retirement*: Put on a new set of tires and keep on going!

---

263 His Harvest (Mission 1000) Newsletter, October 29, 1997.

M/1000 Statistical Overview:[264]

19 three-month sessions over 13 years

220 graduates

52 countries staffed with M/1000 graduates[265] (including):

- Austria
- South Africa
- England
- Belize
- Japan
- India
- Navajo
- Malaysia
- Philippines
- Panama
- Yugoslavia
- Switzerland
- Belarus
- Botswana
- France
- Indonesia
- Kenya
- Martinique
- Nigeria
- Papua New Guinea
- Russia
- Ukraine
- Zambia
- China
- Belgium
- Jamaica
- Germany
- Mexico
- Malawi
- Peru
- Okinawa
- Venezuela

Robin recalled[266] Joe's musings about why he and RB had left Papua New Guinea for Memphis. "Dad said many times, 'It was Memphis because of one man and for one purpose: Larry McKenzie and the vision of Mission 1000.'"

---

264 E-mail from Larry McKenzie (May 2, 2013).

265 M/1000 newsletters state that trainees scattered into 52 countries. I've documented 32 so far.

266 January, 2014 phone interview.

PART 6: RETURN TO OKINAWA (1998-2002)

You might as well suffer rheumatism in India as in Indiana.

Joe Cannon

I GUESS THAT GOES FOR dementia in Okinawa as well.

As Joe and RB's ministry with M/1000 concluded, neither of them wanted to wither away in "retirement." Retirement meant retreat. Joe redefined it to be simply a new direction and vision for mission. By this time Robin and Cyndi had been missionaries themselves in Okinawa for nearly a decade[267] and invited his parents to return to the Okinawan field.

Old soldiers love nothing more than fresh "orders from headquarters." Joe saluted and clicked his heels, as it were, and with RB beside him, they returned to their beloved Okinawa on February 24, 1998. True to his hard-won missionary wisdom, Joe insisted on preparing for himself a five-year strategic plan[268] for a new work in their old and familiar field.

Joe and RB moved into an apartment next door to Robin and Cyndi, effortlessly dusted off their Japanese language skills and set to work. In their first field report, Joe highlighted his responsibilities and endeavors:[269]

---

267 Robin and Cyndi worked in Okinawa from 1989-2001.

268 His Harvest (Mission 1000) Newsletter, January, 1998.

269 Excerpted from June-July and Sept-Oct issues (1998) of *Eastern Light*, the name of their missionary newsletters.

> I preach[ed] monthly for the Logos, Naha, Ishikawa, and Chibana congregations, taught five LST[270] students an hour a week [with each], and wrote "Only To Your Cross I Cling."[271]

The pinnacle of their time in Okinawa was when Joe proudly stood in the gap and covered Robin's various responsibilities while he and Cyndi furloughed for months in the states. Joe and RB were happily in the missionary zone again, but not for long. Sadly, RB's health rapidly declined and soon required round the clock care. Unable to fully serve the ministry, Joe and RB returned to Memphis after only 18 months. Joe informed their supporting churches:

> As you may have already heard, Rosa Belle's dementia has advanced to the point of 24 hour care-giving. I am fully committed to personally caring for her. I consider it a privilege to serve her needs in these latter years as she has served me and our family in 53 years of marriage.

Joe's final field report included this stirring tribute to Rosa Belle:[272]

A WIFE FOR ALL SEASONS

How beautiful you are my darling; Oh how beautiful!

Song of Solomon 4:1

What can I say about the woman who has loved me longer and stronger than any other person? I thank God that our marriage

---

270   LST = Let's Start Talking is a ministry to those interested in learning English as a second language. It is designed to assist language learners toward fluency through one-on-one, cross-cultural friendships by reading together the gospel of Luke to develop vocabulary and grammar skills and to share the gospel of Christ (www.LST.org).

271   I was unable to determine whether this was an article, series of articles, or a book manuscript.

272   *A Wife for All Seasons, His Harvest,* Joe Cannon newsletter (November, 1999). Originally from *The Heart of a Missionary,* (Self-published, 1994, New Zealand).

was made for us in Heaven. I cannot thank her enough or repay her enough for what she means to me. Proverbs 31 is insufficient tribute.

For over forty years we have served the Lord together in missionary work and in the cause of world evangelism. She has uncomplainingly and devotedly followed the leading of our Lord into hard places—right after the war in Japan, then to suffering, war-ravaged Okinawa, to Papua New Guinea, and most recently to the jungles of Irian Jaya. She has endured the cold of Canada and Japan, the heat of the tropics, the hustle and bustle of urban centers, and the isolation of remote mountain outposts.

She has reared seven children, losing one of them in Okinawa. Four of them were adopted from Japan and Korea. She has suffered through operations without anesthesia and has ministered to the medical needs of thousands in our New Guinea clinics.

Her home is always open to travelers, strangers, and journeying missionaries. She has been a mother to single missionaries and a grandmother to missionary children. Her gentle and longsuffering disposition has been a rock, a fortress, and a refuge of strength for her workaholic husband.

Rosa Belle is the best example of a missionary wife that I have ever seen among many wonderful missionary wives. She has nursed me through exhaustion, malaria, dengue fever, operations, diabetes, heart trouble, and many other ailments with faith, patience, and undying love.

She has braved storms at sea, traveled by airplane too often to remember, braved dangers on rivers, mountains, impossible roads, threats from wild men, and exposure to plagues, diseases, and death. Never has she balked at going anywhere or doing anything for Christ. She has more grit in her little finger than most men I know have in their whole bodies. Yet, she is a quiet, unassuming, modest, faithful, and righteous woman. She has lived in all kinds of houses, sheds and huts, eaten all kinds of food, worn all kinds of clothing, and learned to speak all kinds of languages. She knows how to get along without money. When we have money she is never quick to spend it on herself. Her children and grand-children cannot help but love her, and neither can I.

I just want everyone to know that God makes women today as good as he has ever made them, and I am eternally grateful and glad to be happily married to one of them.

In a handwritten version of this same newsletter Joe added:

As for me, I am setting my sights on the future, whatever that may be. I will never voluntarily retire. Not while I have life and breath. . . . I want everyone to know that the vision of Mission/1000 is still alive in me, if not in others. I hope to put the M/1000 para-missionary information on the internet. Also, in our next report I'll tell you about the SOWER[273] program.

ROSA BELLE'S LAST AND LENGTHY TRIAL (2000-2002)

Rosa Belle's health problems became observable in 1996 with recurring short-term memory lapses. The disorder progressed throughout the following year which prompted a family vacation when the diagnosis of dementia was openly recognized and announced. This coincided with the close of Mission 1000 and Joe and RB's brief return to Okinawa in 1999.

While in Okinawa, RB's illness accelerated more quickly than anticipated. The couple's five-year ministry plan was preempted to less than

---

273 Acronym for School of World Evangelism Reapers. Joe envisioned SOWER to be more concentrated than M/1000, a nine-month training regimen focused on cross-cultural awareness and team formation. However, he ran out of life before he could get it established.

two, and they regretfully returned to Memphis. Joe was staunchly loyal to RB and resolved to personally provide for her care himself, which became arguably some of the toughest, most draining work he had ever undertaken. RB's lack of balance and walking difficulties, combined with greatly diminished cognizance abilities, sped along her declining health and threatened to overtake both their lives. By the end of 2000, RB was noticeably weakened and rarely recognized most family members.

Joe and Rosa Belle were firmly anchored by three underpinning pillars that had sustained them during 53 years of marriage and ministry: an unshakeable trust in God, a never-ending romantic marriage, and a resolute ambition to advance the gospel of Christ together. As RB's dementia deepened, a remarkable flurry of prayer journal entries[274] reveal the interplay of these life-mooring mainstays and the life-shattering distress that her slow demise caused for Joe:

> My RB is gradually fading away and can hardly articulate one sentence . . . losing her bit by bit. Lord, have mercy on her and me . . . Is there no future missionary work for us? Help Belarus not to join back with Russia . . . Remove Lukashenko [Belarusian President] from his oppressive power . . . Lord, is there some way we might still go to Indonesia next year? May RB's ill health not reflect badly on the missionary life and the great wife she has been to me [Sept-Dec, 1999].

As RB's illness confined her to a wheelchair, Joe maintained his nearly daily routine of pushing her around the block on two-mile strolls. Joe's journal entries of praise and bosom-buddy petitions to the Lord during these days are stunning:

> Thanks for 70 churches in Japan and Okinawa; 152 congregations in PNG; 12 more in Irian Jaya [Indonesia]. All of them for you Jesus!

---

274 The following interspersed quotations are taken from Joe's personal prayer journals (1999-2002). The words are completely his, though edited for brevity.

A great day for RB. I revel in the encouragement you gave me. Are you starting to heal her? Yes or no, still I will praise your name. Have mercy on RB's old age and mine. Oh Lord, am I finished in missionary work? Where would you have me go next?

During most of 2002, Rosa Belle was immobile and needed to be dressed and hand-fed. Joe was distraught as he watched her slowly retreat into the frightening confusion of no longer recognizing anyone, and he was exhausted by his zealous love and protection of her. Robin recalls his dad saying of those two concluding years, that the "good" days were a "long labor of love" while the "bad" days were endured as a "long, protracted funeral." But he kept praying:

My little best [help] is not much . . . Oh Lord, may your cause prosper in every place that RB and I ever worked for Christ!

My only ambition now is to care for RB into your hands and then pay my last farewell to my overseas brethren. With your permission, may I revisit once more Japan, Okinawa, PNG, Indonesia and Belarus?

RB is getting weaker and I am getting sadder. Please make it easy for her. RB turns 80 today [November 19].

Rosa Belle's physical strength faded throughout November. Near the end, hospice provided friendly care, but was only needed for two days. A wonderful blessing was that Debbie (Cannon) Hogan was in the USA. Robin regularly updated her on their mother's condition. When it was apparent that RB had only a few days to live, Debbie quickly drove to Memphis and was able to arrive about an hour before RB died. Rosa Belle died peacefully surrounded by Joe, Debbie, Robin and Larry McKenzie. Mercifully, the Lord allowed RB to take flight for heaven from her own home on November 22, three days after her 80th birthday.[275]

The journal entries stopped abruptly when Rosa Belle died but started again 12 days later:

> RB is gone. I am devastated. The Lord's will has been done. Blessed be the name of the Lord. This new task [living without RB] I find most formidable. But I turn my life back over to you, yet again, Lord. You know I would like to visit our brethren overseas. Please give me strength to do this.[276]

Forty-five years earlier, on their tenth wedding anniversary, Joe had written a poem for Rosa Belle. Their son, Robin, appropriately recited it during her funeral:[277]

TO THE SWEETEST ROSE OF THEM ALL

Is a rose less a rose,

when in the bud it holds its head up high?

When young and green and strong within

It reaches for the sky?

Is a rose less a rose,

when in full bloom, it glows all afire

in reds and white, in glorious sight

it stands in full attire?

Is a rose less a rose

when it starts to fade,

---

275   Larry McKenzie presided over RB's funeral on November 26, 2002.

276   Joe never did make it back for a visit to Japan, Okinawa, PNG, Indonesia or Belarus.

277   Dated August 28, 1957.

when its work now done, in the evening sun
forward bends in the lengthening shade?

Is a rose less a rose
when the petals fall and the course at last is run?
When it seems to die, with a final sigh,
As it turns to whence it come?

Now it's this we should know
That this rose doth grow, its branch in the living God
'Twas not given in vain, but eternity gains,
When it rises once more from the sod.

PART 7: UKRAINE (2003-2010)

The righteous cry out and the Lord hears them; he delivers them from all their troubles. The Lord is close to the brokenhearted and saves those who are crushed in spirit.[278]

BROKEN PIECES

EXACTLY SIX WEEKS AFTER ROSA Belle's death, Joe poured out his broken heart in his journal:[279]

> I have lost my Rosa Belle, and I don't know what to do. I can't control my tears . . . I only have time for loneliness.

Only five days later, Joe's hope was obviously renewed with this startling announcement:[280]

> Bless Betty Dollar. I asked her to marry me, and she said "Yes." Oh Lord, you are merciful and kind to me and Betty Dollar. May we glorify you together in Ukraine. I am overjoyed—I have a new

---

278 Psalm 34:17-18.

279 Journal entry, January 3, 2003.

280 Journal entry, January 8, 2003.

wife with a new life ahead of us. Lord, please let us live together
long enough to do a lasting work for your glory in Ukraine.

How are we to understand Joe's totally honest, but seemingly opposite, emotional eruptions—less than one week apart?

The Psalm 34 text at the beginning of this section affirms that when the
righteous cry out in despair, the Lord hears, comes near, and delivers the
brokenhearted. Joe was restored by the Lord's faithfulness to His promise.
I am also reminded of the three mainstay pillars that had sustained Joe
and RB for more than 50 years together: 1) a shared and unshakeable faith
in Christ; 2) a romantic marriage partner in ministry; and 3) a resolute
ambition to advance Jesus' name to the ends of the earth.

With no other place to fall, Joe fell upon the rock of his faith in
Christ and his lifelong reason for living, namely to be a ready-to-go
messenger of God's great gospel for the world. The marriage partner
piece was similarly integral to steady Joe's audacious, swashbuckling
persona. Joe needed a wife like peas need a pod.

BETTY DOLLAR CANNON

Betty Pankey was a "Depression baby" born in 1932 in Little Rock,
Arkansas.[281] Her family moved to Memphis, Tennessee, four years
later and attended the Union Avenue Church of Christ. Betty be-
came a believer in Christ as a young girl and was baptized by E.W.
McMillan, one of the founders (along with Joe Cannon) of Ibaraki
Christian College in Japan.

In 1950, at the age of 18, Betty married Dan Dollar, the son of one of
her Sunday School teachers. She began to teach Sunday School classes
for kindergarteners and served as the church secretary. In addition to
Bible teaching, Betty developed Vacation Bible School materials and
wrote instructional books on how to teach preschoolers.

Dan served in the Navy for four years (1952-56) which necessitated
a temporary move away from Memphis. Following that stint in the

---

281 Biographical information confirmed through e-mail exchanges, September 3-6, 2014.

military they adopted two beautiful children, a four-year-old girl (Tina) and a little boy, nearly three (Nim).

Their marriage lasted for three decades but sadly ended in divorce in 1980. Betty acquired her license to sell real estate at age 50, sold six homes in six weeks, and says she "*never* looked back at office work."

Betty's life suddenly took another dramatic twist in June 1994 when she accompanied a team of a dozen people from Highland Church of Christ on a two-week mission trip to Ukraine. She was forever "wrecked" by her love and compassion for the Ukrainian people. During the next year, she closed out her real estate business, endured a bout of breast cancer, and sold her home. She used the money to finance her own ministry over the next seven years[282] in Ukraine.[283] Busy with her career, church activities, and her mission in Ukraine, Betty remained happily single for more than 20 years before becoming acquainted with Joe Cannon.

CAN YOU COOK?

Rosa Belle died in November 2002. Betty had returned stateside from Ukraine for the Christmas holidays and, sometime before Christmas, Larry McKenzie invited Betty to join him and Joe for lunch.[284] Betty had not known Joe and RB, but she had heard of them as missionaries and as the director of Mission 1000. During lunch, Betty expressed her sympathy to Joe on his loss of Rosa Belle. Joe blurted out, "I'm returning to PNG to spend the rest of my life there!" Taken back a bit, she replied, "Good for you, Joe!" Later Joe asked awkwardly, "Can you cook?" Betty replied, "No, not really." And Joe went home.

Betty had scheduled a meeting with the elders on January 5th to discuss direction for future ministry in Ukraine, as she had just turned

---

282   1995-2002.

283   Betty was also financially assisted in Ukraine by the Highland and Ross Road congregations in Memphis and the Brentwood Hills and Whites Creek churches in the Nashville area.

284   The following story was related to me in an audiotaped interview with Joe and Betty in their Memphis home on May 12, 2011.

70 years of age. The following morning Betty was unloading her car, taking groceries into the church building duplex. Joe's house was situated across the street. He looked out his window and muttered, "What a beautiful older lady trying to get her bags out of the car. She's that missionary. I should go over and help her!"

After they unloaded the groceries, Betty offered him a cup of tea. He stayed for three hours hearing about her life, family, and work in Ukraine. Finally, Joe decided that he had to go because his son was hosting a dinner for him that evening. It was his 76th birthday.

Several days later, Larry McKenzie took Joe as a guest to a ladies luncheon. One of the elderly women said, "Brother Cannon, I'm so sorry to know that you're living all alone." Joe retorted, "Well, I'm not going to stay alone. I'm getting married again!" The woman offered her assistance, "Oh, Brother Cannon, there is a nice lady that lives down the road. She's never been married." Joe interrupted her abruptly, "I'll find my own, thank you!"

The next morning, Joe walked across the street to the duplex where Betty was staying. She remembers opening a can of chili and managing not to burn it. "Joe was impressed and thought that was the most wonderful thing." After another hour of chit-chat, Joe declared, "Let's get married, and I'll go to Ukraine. We'll do mission work together!"

Shocked, Betty said "Well, let me think about that and pray on it for a while." She immediately called one of the elders and requested a meeting. In the meantime, she called three other people for advice, and each one commended Joe as a godly man. Betty's own older brother laughed and said, "What have you got to lose, sister?"

Joe moseyed over to the duplex the following morning and said, "Did you see the sunrise this morning? It was orange and silver and was just so beautiful?" Betty concluded, "It just seemed like an answer to prayer, and marrying Joe was the right thing to do."

Such quick pivots were not unusual for Joe, and his children understood his desire to stay busy and to spread the gospel. The suddenness of the decision was understandably difficult, but Joe's family respectfully acquiesced and assisted him in his wedding plans. Five of Joe's six living children came to the wedding. Only Eileen was unable to attend. Joe's oldest son, Joey, served as Best Man and Betty's daughter, Tina Bowie, stood by as her Matron of Honor.

Betty desired a quick and simple wedding in Larry McKenzie's office. But Joe wanted it at the Highland church. One afternoon, he showed her something in his prayer journal (and she confesses to snooping at other things on the page). One of Joe's written prayers was, "Lord, please change Betty's mind so we can get married at Highland church." Betty relented. "If he's got the Lord on his side, I just need to go with it!"

Larry McKenzie was to conduct the wedding service. Even though Joe and Betty had 84 years of wedded experience between them, Larry insisted upon pre-marital counseling. So the three of them, all in their mid-70s, went through the Q & A's of marital counseling together. Evidently, Joe and Betty passed the test because Larry performed the wedding on Saturday afternoon, April 19, 2003, at the Highland church building. The only hiccup in the service was when Joe placed the ring on Betty's finger and deadpanned, "Please don't pawn it!" The crowd didn't hear the remark, but they did see Betty instinctively raise her leg as if to kick Joe. That part is in the wedding video!

Later Joe pranced around the reception boasting of his newfound fortune. "I've never had two cents to rub together, but now I'm 'rolling in the dough.' I'm married to a Dollar!"

Some of Joe's pals plastered shaving cream messages all over the car. The newlyweds drove across Memphis to the Peabody Hotel, a generous gift from one of the Sunday School classes. Joe proudly escorted Betty through the hotel atrium, announcing loudly that they were on their honeymoon and smiling broadly at snickering bystanders. The honeymooners enjoyed two nights and a day at the Peabody Hotel. One month later they landed in Ukraine on Betty's 71st birthday, once again on "front line" mission for Christ and the gospel.

RETURN TO THE FRONT-LINE SMOKE

Whenever Joe was away from what he considered to be the mission field, he grumbled in displeasure about being away from the "front line smoke" of the battlefield. But the exhilaration he enjoyed when personally engaged in mission was palpable. In his first report to their supporters, Joe explained:[285]

> Losing Rosa Belle was the worst experience of my life; having Rosa Belle for 54 years was the best. I was never a despondent person, never brooding, always optimistic, always hopeful. But when loneliness gripped me, I could not shake it off . . . meeting Betty Dollar changed all of that.

> Later this week, before you receive this, we will be off for Ukraine. I'm excited about that! I've been sitting in Memphis spinning my wheels, but now I'll get back on the job I love, namely mission work. New language, new culture, new people, making new disciples, strengthening new churches. It will be great working with Betty, a pioneer missionary who recently became my new wife.

Upon arrival in Ukraine, Joe was "like a mosquito at a nudist colony!" He knew what to do, he just did not know where to start. Though not fluent, he had already studied Russian during the years he and RB worked on short-terms in Belarus.[286] As in every place Joe worked, he aggressively pounced upon language, culture, and local history learning with a fury!

Joe never acquired fluency in either Russian or Ukrainian, but it wasn't for lack of effort. Two things submarined his heroic language efforts. Primarily, his 76-year-old brain simply wasn't the reliable information container it once had been. But also, the Ukrainian people were far more interested in learning English. Even so, Joe coaxed a young brother to exchange daily English lessons for Ukrainian ones. He was so intent on language acquisition that during his first year, he delivered a page-long furlough farewell speech in Ukrainian. Ever the comedian, Joe often joked, "Ukrainian is not so difficult, but you must use your 'Ucranium!'"

---

285 His Harvest Newsletter. *Times of Refreshing* (Acts 3:19), April 2003.

286 Belarus is located on the northern border of Ukraine.

Joe's ministry efforts in Ukraine included the good work of mentoring men, teaching through the Gospels and the book of Revelation, and preaching on many Sundays. He regularly sought to evangelize wherever he was, especially with kids in the orphanage.

Joe and Betty (Dollar) Cannon in Ukraine (2005)

Soon after they settled into her ninth story apartment in Bila Tserkva,[287] Betty took Joe to Shans Center, a boys' and girls' home for those with physical limitations. This orphanage cared for 150 children ages 4-18, most of whom arrived as young children, even infants, and lived there until they graduated from high school. Joe was heart-struck for these disabled kids who were so miserably restricted by crutches or wheelchairs. Even at 76, he was joyfully out on the playground with the younger children playing and horsing around. He did not want to leave them. By rule, they were not supposed to teach "religion," but Joe shared his faith so naturally that no one complained.

When he and Betty got back to their apartment, Joe dreamed up plans to establish a biblically-based orphanage to provide for the material and gospel needs of these children. He also envisioned a school of biblical studies for Ukrainian believers, both male and female. Neither of these ideas materialized as Joe simply ran out of time and energy. However, on Joe and Betty's last Ukraine trip together in 2010, they witnessed the wheelchair-bound son of the director come to faith in Christ and be baptized in a nearby river.

There was a second children's home called the "Boys' House" which supervised Downs Syndrome boys, many of whom had been left at the hospital after birth. These children rarely had visitors and were mostly overseen by female nurses, teachers, and cooks. It was hard to make them happy, but Joe won them over with his fatherly affection and

---

287 A city located 70 miles southwest of Kiev.

Mapping out a strategy for Ukraine and beyond

attention. Joe was observably pleased and content with his regained life as a missionary for Christ:[288]

> I want you all to know that I am immensely happy here. I love the challenge of a new missionary work in a new country . . . I am in good shape and holding up well . . . with periodic check-ups for my heart-valve replacement. I teach Saturday evening Bible studies (Galatians through Colossians) and meet regularly with Kostya Kysilenko, a dynamic preacher of the gospel.

During the seven years that Joe was with Betty in Ukraine, they made a total of 11 trips ranging in length from six months to the last one in 2010, which was only three weeks long.[289]

In the latter years of their work in Ukraine, Joe experienced a more rapid onset of dementia and got lost a couple of times in Bila Tserkva. In July 2010, at the conclusion of a visit from his granddaughter, Jessica,[290] Joe collapsed at the Victoria Station in London, suffering a diabetic seizure. He had just purchased tickets to visit Stonehenge for Jessica's birthday. Medics rushed Joe to a hospital—from which he attempted to escape several times, pushing his IV-stand down the corridors, looking for an exit!

---

288 *His Harvest* missionary newsletter, June, 2003.

289 Betty Dollar Cannon email, August 16, 2014.

290 Story related via phone conversation with Jessica Cannon on August 6, 2014.

PART 8: FINAL DEPARTURE (2011-2012)

"Death alone will put a stop to my efforts!"

David Livingstone (Pioneer Missionary to Africa)

UNTIL 2008, JOE AND BETTY split their time somewhat equally between Memphis and Ukraine. However, during the last two years of that ministry, the Highland elders wouldn't allow them to return during the harsh winters, as the snow and ice posed a frequent hazard.

An added anxiety, largely unspoken, was Joe's decreasing ability to recall and retain information. His combined physical and mental fragility caused concern among his friends, both for his personal well-being and for his capacity to endure the ongoing rigors of cross-cultural mission. The Highland church leadership was appropriately apprehensive about Joe and Betty returning to Ukraine.

But who was going to tell Joe that he could not return to the mission field?

FAITHFULNESS

Following two bouts with diabetic comas and suffering from physical exhaustion, Joe was home in Memphis but, in his 83-year-old mind, he still had unfinished business in Ukraine. When asked how he felt, his standard reply was, "I'm tired. But I can be tired in Ukraine. Let's get back to it!"

Betty does not remember a definitive decision being made by the elders that she and Joe could not return to the field. It was the passage of time that made the decision for them. Joe no longer had the physical or mental energies to make arduous worldwide jaunts.

In May 2011, the Highland Church of Christ honored Joe, Betty, and the memory of RB with a celebration of Joe's nearly 65 years of missionary service[291] in Japan, Okinawa, PNG, and Ukraine. The article *Tribute to Faith* asked, "What would possess a couple to do this (spend 60 plus years overseas preaching the gospel)?" Joe answered the question in a previously written newsletter in which he described what he loved most about the missionary life:[292]

> Pioneering with the gospel! This is the great thrill of missionary work . . . bringing souls to Christ who have never heard of Him . . . In mission, you go by faith into the unknown. You bet your life on the promises and providence of God . . . What a joy to this happy pioneer to arrive in strange places and find Christ is there . . . To meet the challenges, to have every fiber of your soul tested and tried. To be purified by the ups and downs, the successes and failures, the joy and sorrow . . . To be in the place where gospel victories are won against seeming overwhelming odds. What can take the place of experiences like that? This is the life for me!

FORCED RETIREMENT

I traveled through Memphis in September 2011 to visit Joe and Betty. I was on mission to gather materials and conduct interviews with as

---

291   I was unable to confirm the date of the tribute. However, Candace Goff, Communications Specialist at Highland Church wrote an article, *Tribute to Faith* (May 21, 2011) in the *Commercial Appeal* newspaper, Memphis, TN.

292   Quoted from *Tribute to Faith, Commercial Appeal* (May 21, 2011), Memphis, TN. Original source unknown.

many as possible, in preparation for writing this book.[293] As the three of us talked, mostly Betty and me with Joe listening, I asked if they had plans to return to Ukraine.

Betty hemmed and hawed a bit and finally replied, "Well, it looks like the elders consider us to be *retired*." My ears perked up like a rat smelling cheese! "Retired?" I said, immediately thinking of all the times Joe had vowed to "never retire" and that he would "die in harness!" I asked Betty, "How has Joe taken *that* news?" She whispered, "He hasn't taken it yet!"

I then turned and spoke directly to Joe, baiting him a little. "Joe, you told me in the 1970s that you would never retire! How do you feel about the elders not letting you go back to the field?" His eyes popped open like he had just leapt out of a coma! He inched forward to the edge of his chair, sucked his cheeks full of air and sputtered, "*Pfffewwwtt!* Let the elders retire! I'll have none of it! C'mon brother, we can still do it!"

He looked around the room as though searching for his backpack. Then he stretched his arm out, pointed to his bedroom and snorted,

"I'M NOT GOING TO DIE IN A HOSPICE BED.
I WANT TO BE SHOT OUT OF THE SADDLE!"

After he calmed down, I asked him to sit on the couch beside me. "Joe, people say that if we keep going to New Guinea (dangerous places) that we're going to 'lose our lives.' What do you say?"

"*Impossible!*" he said. "We gain our lives when we go. And if they kill us, we gain our lives even quicker! But yes, there is danger and a lot of dying to self, but God met with us, didn't he, brother? I can't get over how the Lord worked with us. I don't want to get over it. I'll never get over it. It's wonderful!"

David Sitton with Joe (September, 2011)

---

293 Thankfully, most of the following conversation (and much more) is on audio tape.

Joe looked me eye to eye and said, "You're a queer!" Before I could recover from his use of that word, he continued, "You're a misfit! You and me, we are 'great commissioners!' And we'll be great commissioners until we die! But until then we gotta do something about it. We've gotta move our feet. We've gotta be 'on the go and raise the dough' and raise the hackles on the brethren's hide!"

I thought of the song *Hard Fighting Soldier* and blurted out the first line. He joined in and we clumsily sang the verse together. [294] Afterward Joe exclaimed, "That's it! That's our song, brother! Heaven is where I belong and the sooner the better!" These were great and memorable hours with Joe.

Countless times over the previous six decades, Joe had slipped a $20, $50, or $100 dollar bill into the palm or shirt pocket of a financially struggling missionary. He did so with me several times through the years. (To the end, Joe was fiercely compelled by his passion for Christ, his compassion for lost souls, and the profound camaraderie of front-line soldiers who had struggled and scraped through hard times together for the spread of the gospel.) Even on this day as I prepared to leave, he yelled to Betty to bring some money to give me. I said, "Joe, I'm not taking any money from you. I don't need it, and I don't want it." He persisted in pressing some bills into my hand, but I persisted harder and, for once, refused the money.

It was not easy for me to hug Joe because he was so tall, but I hugged him anyway and kissed him on his forehead. That was the last time I was with him except during his final hours on his hospice bed.

Joe and Betty enjoyed a good last year together.[295] He was fairly strong and delighted in playing his accordion and spending time with his grandchildren when he had opportunities. A month before he died, in the middle of the night, an ambulance rushed Joe to the hospital where he stayed for three weeks. From there, he was moved to hospice. Joe would spend only five days there before making his final journey to where he most wanted to go.[296]

---

294 The two of us singing is on tape. A woefully inept, but joyful, rendition!

295 Betty Cannon e-mail (August, 2014).

296 Joe died about 6:00 A.M. on Oct. 25, 2012. Following his funeral at Highland

LAST CALL

Don't cry for me at my funeral, pal, because I'll be
crying for you poor schmoes.

Joe Cannon

To Every Tribe[297] had scheduled our Ekballo Mission Conference in Olive Branch, Mississippi,[298] and I was already en route when the call came from Robin that his dad was near the end of life. I arrived in Memphis the following morning to visit him as he lay in his hospice bed.

Dave Hogan, Joe's son-in-law, was sitting with him when I arrived. After a while, Dave excused himself and left me alone with him. Joe was reclined in his bed, connected to both oxygen and an IV. His head was tilted back, eyes closed. He was breathing noisily but peacefully. I sat quietly and held his hand.

This was, I realized, my final opportunity to say something. I leaned over him, our faces only inches apart, and spoke loudly into his ear:

> "Joe, I don't know if you can hear me, but this is David Sitton. I used to work with you in Papua New Guinea." His hand twitched. "You're getting ready to go to Heaven, brother! And I just want you to know that[299] 'It has always been my ambition to preach the gospel [*He held my hand in a strong grip, his moist eyes opened slightly, and his back lifted off the bed rocking hard back and forth as I quoted the verse*] . . . where Christ was not known, so that I would not be building on someone else's

---

Church (Cordova) on Oct. 27, he was buried at Memphis Memory Gardens. He is survived by wife, Betty Dollar Cannon; children – Eileen, Joseph, Deborah, Leonard, Gregory, and Robin; stepchildren – Tina Bowie and Nim Underwood; and 18 grandchildren and 7 great-grandchildren.

297 To Every Tribe was founded by David Sitton in 2004. www.toeverytribe.org.

298 A city near Memphis.

299 This is the text (Romans 15:20-21) he quoted to me in 1977 when he passionately challenged me to join him in the PNG mission.

foundation . . . but those who were not told about him will see, and those who have not heard will understand.' I'm going to continue that work, Joe!"

He visibly relaxed back onto the bed.

As family members arrived and rotated in and out, spending their final hours with him, I retreated to the waiting room, joyful that the Lord had graced me with those brief moments.

Within 15 hours Joe was with Christ where—if possible—he was crying for the rest of us "poor schmoes" he had left behind.

EPILOGUE: THE OUTSIDE MAN

He was one of our best men in the bush . . .

Sir John Hubert Murray about Jack Hides

THE "OUTSIDE MEN" WERE THE roughest, toughest, and gruffest of Sir John Hubert Murray's famed troop of patrol officers during the early settling of the Territory of New Guinea in the 1930s and 40s. These men heartily opened the remotest parts of the island, nearly barehanded, facing down huge mountains, treacherous rivers, and fierce tribesmen. In many ways, the outside men were *trail-blazers*. They didn't *follow* trails; they *carved* them out of jungles. In his prologue to *The Outside Man: Jack Hides of Papua,* James Sinclair describes Jack Hides, perhaps the most renowned of the early New Guinea colonizers:[300]

> He was one of a breed of men who have ever been reckless of danger and risk; a breed uncommon, courageous, difficult to assess by the standards of ordinary men. A man of strange qualities, a romantic, a dreamer, always straining to see what lay on the far side of the hill. A man of decided abilities and evident faults . . . A man who walked the formidable mountains of untamed Papua.

---

300 James Sinclair. *The Outside Man: Jack Hides of Papua* (Lansdowne Press, Melbourne, 1969), page xiii.

Like Jack Hides, Joe Cannon was an *outside man:* fearless, bold, brash, undaunted, unconventional, unpredictable, playfully inappropriate at times, and unapologetically controversial—but all for Christ and the gospel. Joe (also like Hides) was prone to exercise a stubborn streak and was terribly impatient with certain types of people. Though well aware of his shortcomings, he downplayed them by unpretentiously leading with his strengths: vision, charisma, initiative, physical energy, and endurance.

Whether preaching, praying, or instigating rambunctious jesting among buddies, Joe was fun to listen to (and observe). When he preached, his hands flailed around like a shadow-boxer as he maneuvered around the platform. Whether in or out of the pulpit, he could deliver hard truths with a humorous uppercut. In New Guinea when his good friend Ray Lock whined about not having enough money to take a vacation with his family, Joe got tired of hearing it and quipped, "Ray, you're an accountant! How much does a nervous breakdown cost? Find the

Joe Cannon, ". . . Our best man in the bush"

money and go give *me* a rest!" Ray laughed and found a way to get away for a much-needed holiday.

Like the old-time outside men before them, Joe and RB were self-reliant and cheerfully menial. They lived in tin sheds, slept under land cruisers during thunderstorms, endured serious illnesses without fanfare, and scrubbed the nastiest village outhouses for their teams to use.

Finally, Joe was fearless, even when making mistakes. He had such sincerity about him that, when he screwed up, he was the first to know it and the first to try to repair the damage and learn from it. Joe's humility, brash as it seemed at times, greatly endeared him to the national brothers. They learned to imitate his hard following after Christ and his speed at repenting and moving on after their own blunders. Like the early disciples, the original outside men, Joe lived crossways with his own culture. He dwelled in another kingdom and served a greater King.

JOE'S DREAM REVEALED

You can work without praying, but it is a bad plan.

Hudson Taylor (Missionary to China)

For reasons unknown to me, Joe never intended for his most cherished aspiration to become bandied about in public. Apparently, it was simply a private conversation between him and the Lord. In all of his missionary strategizing, he never mentioned it (to my knowledge), except in widely scattered notations through nearly 60 years of his personal prayer journals, i.e. *"Remember the dream, Lord."*[301]

During the 1980s he often referenced, more specifically, the number 10,000.

Mission 10,000, for the lost world![302]

---

301 March 15 and 28, 1984 journal entries.

302 July 12, 1984 journal entry.

MAY 10,000 BE FIELDED FOR CHRIST[303]

and 10,000 to arise for the harvest![304]

So Joe prayed through the decades. What was the compelling vision that endured through almost six decades of Joe's frequently recorded petitions and intercessions? Here it is, said best in this March 10, 2002 entry:

> Missionaries, Lord! Send forth more [10,000] of them, I beg, O Lord of the harvest!

Joe's laser-focused request was that God would propel 10,000 pioneer church-planting missionaries into the unreached harvest fields of the world.

THE RIGHT KIND OF MISSIONARY

They did not love their lives so much as to shrink from death.[305]

Unsown frontiers require long-haul, hard-slogging seed-sowers, and one must not get the harvesting combine ahead of the seed bag. Uncultivated fields are not yet "ready for the picking," but rather for the plowing. So it is with un-evangelized lands. The testimony of a farmer is one of persistent plowing, planting, watering, weeding, and nurturing. Then, "at the proper time we will reap a harvest if we do not give up."[306]

Shovels (hard work), seed (the Word of God) and water buckets (prayer) are the tools of a gospel pioneer. Joe relished this kind of laborer who, like Epaphroditus to Paul, could become a trusted

---

303 September 4, 1985 journal entry.

304 October 3, 1985 journal entry.

305 Revelation 12:11.

306 Galatians 6:9.

"brother, fellow-worker and fellow-soldier . . . who almost died, risking his life for the gospel."[307]

There is still pioneer plowing to be done for the gospel, but it will not be finished by rubberneckers who are always on the lookout for an easier field. Joe exuded the indispensable perseverance of the plowman who did not look back once his hand was on the till and his eyes were fixed upon the furrow.

To return to one of Joe's favorite analogies: Spearheads pierce targets! Spears are violent weapons specially crafted to destroy targets. A *gospel spearhead*[308] is a spiritually violent person[309] who penetrates enemy territory and the demonic entrapments that have strangled unreached peoples for centuries. Warfare imagery is an apt biblical depiction of what happens when gospel light crashes head on with demonic darkness. Far more than a mere bump of cultures, this is a hell-shattering collision of kingdoms! Warfare lingo such as this assumes conflict and casualties. This is a sure reality for gospel warriors. If we don't intend that implication, we should talk about recruiting gospel *beanbags*[310] instead! Advancing the gospel into hostile territory is not for the faint of frame or faith.

Joe was an exceptional visionary, though more than a few supposed he was a bit hare-brained[311] in his convictions. Everyone agreed, though, that he was a leader who made things happen. Joe was an indefatigable missionary mobilizer. In every field in which he labored, he was in full-steam-ahead, prayer and recruitment mode for additional laborers. He

---

307 Philippians 2:25, 30

308 Psalm 127:4-5 is an example of Scripture using metaphors of an "arrow" and "warfare" to describe spiritual battle; see also Ephesians 6:16.

309 Do not misunderstand the metaphor. Gospel spearheads are violent toward hell, not human beings (Ephesians 6:12; 2 Corinthians 10:3-5). When spiritual conflict becomes physical, such as during persecution, followers of Jesus are to react as lambs receiving the violence, not militants inflicting it (Luke 10:3).

310 A comfortable body pillow; a large bag filled with high-density Styrofoam beads which produces a comfortable foam chair to lounge on.

311 "Crazy; foolish; wild and/or unbalanced."

playfully referred to it as "gunning for game" for which he didn't need a hunting license! I doubt he ever met a believer that he didn't directly challenge for mission work. Joe was keen to use anyone the Lord sent his way. Trusting that many of them would turn into ambassadorial arrows for the grace of God, he eagerly gave them opportunities "to give it a go."

For nearly 65 years, Joe regularly used spearheading imagery to purposely rattle security-addicted Western Christianity and cause believers to "count the cost of the Great Commission." Joe's rallying call for pioneer spearheads to boldly go into all the world and preach the gospel was exhilarating. Thousands were roused by that challenge, and hundreds have found their way to missionary frontlines because of his influence.

The world did not pause for a moment when Joe Cannon died. There was little mention of it, even in local newspapers. But, heaven noticed.[312] No doubt there was (or will be) a long line of very odd-looking, strange-sounding individuals who will escort him into heaven. I can only imagine the sound and sight of all the hooting, hollering, and back-slapping! Those *believers* will be there by the grace of God and because of the love of one who cared enough to give his life to get the gospel preached to them.

Joe's legacy lives. It is extended and multiplied through his spiritual children and grandchildren: Japanese, Okinawan, Papua New Guinean, Indonesian, and Ukrainian—and all those they will continue to reach.

It has been my pleasure to write Joe's story, and it is one of my highest joys that he considered me to be "one of his boys."

---

312 Psalm 116:15.

ENDNOTES

I List of Churches that Ceased Meeting (25 Total)

Enga Province
Lokaitas
Kubin
Wabag
Maramuni

Western Highlands
Iki
Gumanch
Bagalaga
Dumkola
Oglepup

Southern Highlands
Gihamu
Mendi
Tari
Maipini

Balk
Koltum
Wara Kagl
Kobuga
Minip

Chimbu
Wara Bota
Bima

Minj
Ulya
Kiripiya
Baisu
Wara Magwa

II PNG National Evangelist and Missionary List: Compiled by David Sitton, Rick Niland, and Larry Voyles

Ate Miopa
Ate Tapas
Councilman Dai
Councilman Karapin
Devit Berim
Devit Isawe
Garoa Sumagau
Isak
Jab Mesa
Jon Kau
Jon Kerenga
Joss Aiep
Kamosano
Kwotoloko
Malatakamaso
Markus Pup
Miamel Golabe

Limb Jekop
Neme Mile
Peter Lumbura
Robert Mingo
Robin Gabora
Silas Kazo
Simon Gerel
Sombo Dowara
Tanike Pimbin
Teo
Tine Bessi
Wesley Wosse
Woponoko Kosamolco
Yawe
Yusi Miopa
Zonzo

III PNG Missionary List (last name, first name):

Anderson, Evelyn Blount
Ataka, Hideki
Bailey, Garry
Bently, Barry and Sheri
Bingham, Bob
Bowman, Mel and Donna
Broom, Kathryn
Bunt, Tom and Rens
Burrows, Fred and Sandy
Cannon, Joe and Rosa Belle

Lewis, Hank
Lifsey, Phil and Nancy
Lock, David and Karen
Lock, Mike and Barbie
Lock, Ray and Elizabeth
McAnally, Paul and Linda
McGeachy, Jim and Bessie
McMillan, Dave and Heather
Moore, Martha
Moore, Tom and Kathy

Chance, Janie
Church, Kathy
Coles, Reg and Ruth
Conway, Larry
Cope, Janet
DiGiorgio, Joe and Diane
Dowden, Kent and Marinell
Downing, Bruce and Leslea
Dye, Kevin and Tammie
Fairley, Lorna
Farmer, Glenn
Forman, Velma
Ford, Art and Ruby
Ford, Craig and Jeri
Franklin, Willie and Pam
Friis, Lance
Fucudo, Kiyoko
Gelley, Florence
Goldsmith, Gordon and Ruth
Hammond, Guy
Harrison, Curtis and LaMoine
Henderson, Alan and Lanita
Henderson, Robin
Herndon, Bob and Millie
Hoover, Pat
Huff, Tobey and Kathy
Hyer, Gary and Vickie
Jackson, Andrew and Maggie
Johnson, Fran
Johnston, Irene
Kennedy, Jim and Jerrie
Kirkpatrick, Sam and Margaret

Morgan, Duane and Carol
Morgan, Rex and Brenda
Moriarty, Jason
Muller, Angela
Murphree, John and Cornelia
Niland, Rick and Ruth
Ogle, Laura
Oksaka, Nagisa
Orr, Marilyn
Page, Ken and Lois
Reese, Marcus and Diane
Reynolds, Joe and Rhenel
Saito, Etsuko
Scott, Andy and Catherine
Scott, Michael
Shaw, Sally
Sims, Joe and Jane
Sitton, David and Tommi
Stidworthy, Pati
Square, Woody and Judy
Suzuki, Teruko
Templeton, Dale
Voyles, Larry and Lois
Wallace, John and Sara
Warren, Sam and Joni
Williams, Les and Loopie
Willis, T.J.
Wills, Tim
Zimmerman, Ruth

ABOUT THE AUTHOR

David Sitton, carried only a Bible, a suitcase and a surfboard when he set off for Papua New Guinea on October 3, 1977. For thirty-eight years the Lord has lead him to spearhead the gospel into remote and un-reached peoples of Papua New Guinea and Southern Mexico.

Now through the ministry of *To Every Tribe*, he continues to take fresh aim upon new gospel targets in northern India, Indonesia and First Nations Canada peoples as well as continuing the work In Papua New Guinea and Mexico.

David and his wife, Tommi, work with a great team of old and young missionaries to mobilize the church, equip new laborers for the front-lines and launch pioneer church planting teams to the ends of the un-reached earth.

For more information about
David Sitton
&
Hard Fighting Soldier
please visit:

toeverytribe.org
david.sitton@toeverytribe.org
@davidsitton
@toeverytribe
www.facebook.com/davidsitton
www.facebook.com/toeverytribe

For more information about
AMBASSADOR INTERNATIONAL
please visit:
www.ambassador-international.com
@AmbassadorIntl
www.facebook.com/AmbassadorIntl